STARTING SENSORY THERAPY

Fun Activities for the Home and Classroom!

BONNIE ARNWINE

**Fun Activities for the Home
and Classroom!**

All marketing and publishing rights guaranteed to and reserved by
Sensory World, 1010 N. Davis St, Arlington, TX 76012.

Sensory World
info@sensoryworld.com
www.sensoryworld.com
(877) 775-8968
(682) 558-8941
(682) 558-8945 (fax)

Book design by Composure Graphics
Cover and interior by Composure Graphics

ISBN-13: 978-1-935567-26-4

To my husband, Geoffrey Arnwine, who encouraged me to write this book because he believed it would help other parents.

Table of Contents

Acknowledgments

In a way, one could say this book has been in development for centuries. It is a collection of activities that caregivers have passed down for many years. I would like to begin by acknowledging this creative and collective spirit. By freely sharing their successes, past educators continue to shape and develop our children. For my part, this book has been a work in progress for the past 15 years. It began when I started playing with my son.

Many people had a role in this book's development. I would like to start by thanking the staff at First Presbyterian Church Preschool. You helped me find services for my son, gave me a great job, shared with me many of the fun activities within this book, and encouraged me when times were tough. I love you!

Lori J. Davids, OTR, and Joan Reuveni introduced me to the world of Sensory Processing Disorder and patiently taught me how to help my son. You are both excellent practitioners and advocates. Your work improved the quality of my family's life forever. Words cannot express my thankfulness.

Finally, I want to acknowledge my two children—Geoffrey and Grace. I would never have written this book without them. They have opened up a new world for me, and I am a better person because of them.

Introduction

Chances are, if you're reading this book, it's because you have a child or work with a child who has Sensory Processing Disorder (SPD). This book is not filled with in-depth explanations or checklists designed to evaluate SPD. What it's filled with is lots of fun and inexpensive sensory activities that can be set up and cleaned up quickly in your home or facility. It also contains information on how to get help for a child with SPD.

Each chapter contains activities based on a sensory need. All activities require only common household items. "Extend It!" ideas are also included to extend a child's interest. After all, there is nothing worse than setting up a project that only holds a child's interest for 2 or 3 minutes! My son and I spent countless hours enjoying the activities in this book. I hope you and the children you work with will enjoy them, too.

The Terms We Use to Describe Sensory Processing Disorder

In 2004, a committee of occupational therapists clarified the terms we use to describe sensory problems. The committee included Lucy Jane Miller, PhD, OTR, FAOTA; Sharon A. Cermak, EdD, OTR/L, FAOTA; Shelly J. Lane, PhD, OTR/L, FAOTA; and Marie E. Anzalone, ScD, OTR, FAOTA; as well as Beth Osten, OTR; and Stanley I. Greenspan, MD.

This chart, which shows the various types of SPD, illustrates the many ways that the disorder can manifest itself in children. These subtypes of SPD can occur in any combination, resulting in a very wide range of symptoms.

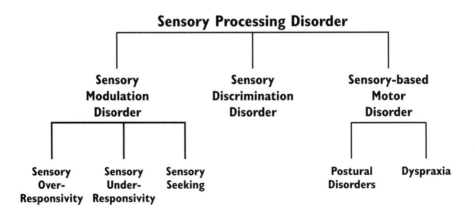

CHAPTER I

OUR SENSES

Sensory Processing Disorder (SPD) is a neurological disorder that causes the brain to misunderstand information it receives from the senses. This causes people with SPD to respond inappropriately to ordinary sensory experiences. Normal sensory experiences can be painful or frightening to them. People with SPD often have difficulty making their bodies do what they want them to do. These sensory difficulties often disrupt daily life and can cause difficulties for the whole family. The degree and severity of SPD is different for each person.

In order to understand SPD, we need to understand the purpose of our senses. Our senses allow us to experience and respond to our environment. To experience a sunset, we look at it. If we smell smoke, we respond by getting out of the building. When our senses are working together properly, they protect us and allow us to enjoy our surroundings. The five senses most of us are familiar with are:

- *Vision,* or visual perception
- *Hearing,* or auditory perception
- *Touch,* or tactile perception
- *Smell,* or olfactory perception
- *Taste,* or oral perception

Two senses we may not be familiar with are:

- *Vestibular,* or sensory information we receive from our middle ear that is related to movement and balance. As a child, did you ever spin yourself in circles and then try to walk straight? You couldn't walk straight because your body was receiving impaired vestibular information.

- *Proprioceptive,* or sensory information we receive from our muscles, joints, and body parts. Close your eyes, and raise your hand in the air. Even though you're not looking at it, you know where your hand is because the muscles and joints in your hand and arm are sending information to your brain, telling it the position of your hand.

These seven senses work together to help us understand and maneuver within our environment. For example, to open a door:

- We look at it by using our visual perception.
- We place our hand on the doorknob by using our visual and tactile perception.
- We squeeze the doorknob (not too hard or too soft) and turn it by using our tactile and proprioceptive perception.
- We pull the door open (not too hard or too soft) by using our vestibular, proprioceptive, visual, and tactile perception.
- If the door has a squeaky hinge, we hear it as we open it by using our auditory perception.
- We walk through the doorway and step over the doorjamb by using our visual, vestibular, and proprioceptive perception.

If the brain is receiving inaccurate sensory information, someone may:

- Bump into the door.
- Slam the door.
- Hit himself with the door.
- Trip or bang into the doorway as he walks through it.
- Be unable to open the door.

SPD has three major subtypes: sensory modulation disorder, sensory-based motor disorder, and sensory discrimination disorder.

Sensory Modulation Disorder

Sensory modulation disorder causes a person's body to misinterpret the nature and intensity of sensory information he or she receives from the environment. One or more of a person's senses may be over- or underresponsive to sensory information. This can also cause a person to crave or seek out sensory stimulation.

Overresponsivity

If a person is overresponsive to sensory stimulation, he or she may have a tendency to respond to certain harmless sensations as if they are dangerous or painful. He may:

- Avoid letting people touch him.
- Become agitated if a peer accidentally bumps him.
- Scream during hair washing or brushing.
- Gag or avoid certain textures of food.
- Scream or cover his ears if he hears a vacuum cleaner running or a dog barking.
- Fear ordinary movement activities, like swings, slides, or ramps.

Underresponsivity

Individuals with sensory underresponsivity do not feel stimulation at the same intensity that typically developing individuals feel it. They may need an extended duration of stimulation, more frequent stimulation, or more intense administration of stimulation to get the same sensation that a typically developing person has. He may:

- Underrespond to pain, getting a cut, or bruising.
- Chew on inedible objects, such as clothing, toys, or objects he finds on the ground (wood chips, sand, or sticks).
- Bump or crash into things.

- Tire easily.
- Avoid contact with others.

Sensory Seeker

A child who is a sensory seeker literally craves sensory experiences. These kids often look for ways to meet their sensory needs that are not socially acceptable. Children who are sensory seekers may:

- Turn the TV volume up extremely high.
- Constantly crash into things.
- Enjoy roughhousing.
- Constantly seek out things to touch.
- Fidget or find it impossible to sit still.
- Lick, chew, or suck on their shirts or other nonfood items.

A Combination of Responses

Typically, a person with sensory modulation disorder has a combination of modulation responses to sensory stimulation. For example, a child may be a sensory seeker and crave oral stimulation and constantly chew her clothing, while at the same time she's underresponsive to touch (and therefore unmotivated to move or play) and overresponsive to noise (so that she covers her ears and screams every time the vacuum cleaner is turned on). SPD looks different for every child.

Furthermore, the way a child responds to her environment can change, depending on fatigue, changes in her routine, or any number of additional factors.

Sensory Discrimination Disorder

A child with sensory discrimination disorder has difficulty understanding the *quality* of sensory information he is receiving from his environment. It can be difficult for him to tell the difference between similar sensations. Children with sensory discrimination disorder may:

- Have trouble distinguishing the difference between similar sounds—for example, the words "rack" and "back" may sound exactly the same to them.

- Not understand what they are touching without looking at it. For example, if they place their hands in a paper bag, they may not be able to tell the difference between a small toy and a marble without looking at it.

- Appear awkward or clumsy.

- Have difficulty recognizing the difference between various smells, tastes, or textures of foods.

Sensory-based Motor Disorder

Children with sensory-based motor disorder have problems making their bodies do what they want them to do. These children have difficulty responding appropriately to proprioceptive and vestibular information they receive from their environment. Remember that the proprioceptive sense provides information we receive from our muscles and joints that helps us understand what our bodies are doing and the positions of our body. The vestibular sense pertains to balance, to help us understand where our body is in relationship to the earth. When these two senses aren't working together, it is difficult for a person to make his body respond effectively to his environment.

The two subtypes of sensory-based motor disorder are dyspraxia and postural disorder.

Dyspraxia

A child with dyspraxia has difficulty imagining, coordinating, and executing movement. Dyspraxia can involve gross-motor, fine-motor, or oral-motor skills, or a combination of all three. Children with dyspraxia may:

- Trip often and appear clumsy.

- Bump into people, break things, and seem accident prone.

- Have problems with chewing and eating or have a tendency to drool.

- Have trouble with dressing, grooming, or self-care.

- Have difficulty holding a pencil or finishing an assignment that involves multiple steps to complete.

Postural Disorder

Children with postural disorder tend to have poor muscle tone. These kids have trouble meeting the demands of common daily tasks. Children with postural disorder may:

- Have difficulty attending to tasks.

- Often seem fatigued.

- Have difficulty sitting up straight.

- Have a poor sense of balance and fall over. They may even fall off their seats.

- Have sloppy or unreadable handwriting.

As you can see, SPD is a complex condition. To assess SPD accurately, a series of assessments must be conducted by a knowledgeable professional. This person is usually an occupational therapist or, in some cases, an adaptive physical education specialist.

Getting Your Child Evaluated

If your child exhibits these types of behaviors but has not received an official diagnosis of SPD, he or she must be evaluated. Ask your pediatrician for a referral. Your pediatrician should have a good understanding of your insurance coverage and referral services through your local school district or early intervention agency. If your pediatrician does not "believe in" SPD or does not want to make a referral to a specialist, find another pediatrician who will work with you.

What Does an Evaluation Look Like?

Evaluations are usually performed by an occupational therapist and can take place at an early intervention center, local school, hospital, or private clinic. Before the initial evaluation, parents and teachers are usually given a questionnaire to fill out. The questions are designed to gauge the child's response to various sensory experiences. This will help the therapist to prepare appropriate activities ahead of time, to get the most out of the evaluation.

On the day of the evaluation, make sure the child is well rested. Plan to arrive early, to allow plenty of time for the therapist to get an accurate picture of the child's abilities. During the evaluation, it may look like the therapist is just playing with the child. However, this is play with a purpose. Actually, the therapist is evaluating the child's gross-motor, fine-motor, oral-motor, and visual-perception skills to see if the child has reached appropriate developmental milestones.

During the evaluation, the therapist will provide a variety of sensory experiences and evaluate the child's responses to them. Usually, the therapist will take notes or check things off a list so that he or she can create a detailed report. The child may stack blocks, draw or color, eat a snack, play with play dough, swing, go down a slide, walk upstairs, or try to mimic the movements of the therapist.

At the end of the evaluation, the therapist will usually ask if you have any questions, or he or she may have a few additional questions for you or your child's teacher to answer. Depending on how the child feels, for example if he or she became overstimulated or fatigued, the therapist may set up an additional evaluation time.

When the written evaluation is complete, the therapist will set up a meeting time to go over the report, answer any questions you may have, and make suggestions for treatment. If possible, ask the therapist to provide you with a copy of the report before the meeting. This will give you an opportunity to review the report and write down any questions you have about it before you meet. Now is the time to ask lots of questions. Also, if you have a concern that hasn't been mentioned, now is the time to talk about it. Remember, no question is a dumb question! It's vital that everyone feels confident about understanding every aspect of the evaluation and suggested interventions.

Getting Therapy for Your Child

If the child is at least 3 years old and qualifies for special-education services, he or she may be eligible for therapy through the local school district. If your child is younger than 3 years, he or she may receive services through your state's early intervention program. Unfortunately, at the time of this writing, SPD is not a part of the *Diagnostic and Statistical Manual of Mental Disorders* (a listing of psychiatric disorders and their corresponding diagnostic codes). This can make it difficult to get services if your child does not have a coexisting condition, such as autism. Some insurance providers will cover the initial evaluation and occupational therapy sessions with a sensory-integration focus.

Services through an Insurance Company

Insurance plans may provide coverage for occupational therapy with a sensory-integration approach. However, each insurance plan is different, so you will have to investigate your coverage. The following is a list of helpful insurance codes according to the International Classification of Diseases system, or ICD:

ICD-9 Diagnostic Codes	
279.11	DiGeorge syndrome
299.0	Autism
299.8	Pervasive developmental disorder, Asperger syndrome
314.0	Attention-deficit disorder
314.01	Attention-deficit/hyperactivity disorder
315.4	Developmental coordination disorder, dyspraxia
315.8	Delay in development (specified)
315.9	Delay in development (unspecified)
343.9	Cerebral palsy

continued

ICD-9 Diagnostic Codes *continued*	
348.3	Encephalopathy
349.9	Unspecified disorders of the nervous system
382.9	Otitis media
742.9	Unspecified anomaly of the brain, spinal cord, and nervous system
759.83	Fragile X syndrome
781.3	Lack of coordination—dyspraxia
784.69	Motor apraxis
782.0	Disturbance of skin sensation
781.0	Tremors, nervous system

Treatment Codes Related to Occupational Therapy (CPT Codes for Billing)

97110	Therapeutic procedure—develop strength/endurance, range of motion
97112	Neuromuscular reeducation—balance, coordination, proprioception
97530	Therapeutic activities—improve functional performance
97533	Sensory-integration techniques
97535	Self-care/activities of daily living (ADLs) training
97770	Self-care/home management

Services Provided through the Local School District: The IEP Process

Before your child starts receiving services through the local school district, you will have to obtain an individualized education plan (IEP). An IEP is a federally mandated education plan that is individualized for every child with a disability. In developing an IEP, educators work with administrators and parents to develop a plan (in the form of goals) to help a child learn. An IEP looks different for each person. Each IEP must contain the following information:

- *Current performance:* The IEP must state how the child is currently doing. This information usually comes from tests, evaluations, and observations made by parents, teachers, therapists, and other school staff.

- *Annual goals:* These are goals that the IEP team believes the child can reasonably accomplish in a year. Goals are broken down into short-term objectives or benchmarks. Goals can be academic, social, or behavioral; relate to physical needs; or address other educational needs.

- *Special-education and related services:* The IEP must list any services that are necessary to help the child meet his or her IEP goals.

- *Participation with nondisabled children:* The IEP must explain the extent (if any) to which the child will not participate with typically developing children in regular class activities and other school activities.

- *Participation in state- and district-wide tests:* The IEP must state what modifications, if any, the child will need regarding the administration of tests. If a proposed testing method is not appropriate for the child, the IEP must state why the method is not appropriate and how the child will be tested instead. Accommodations can be changes to the design of the test, the way a child will answer, the setting, the timing, or the scheduling. Remember, the goal of these tests is to measure knowledge, not *how* someone takes a test. Some examples of accommodations include:

  - A child with poor fine-motor skills may have difficulty filling in the bubbles of a Scantron form, so he or she is allowed to circle answers directly on the test itself.

  - A child with sensitive hearing can take his test in a quiet area, away from noise.

- A child with poor executive functioning may write answers directly on a test or have the assistance of an aid to correctly place his answers on a form.

- A child with substantial language delays may be tested by using multiple choice, rather than being asked to write out short answers.

- A child with auditory processing issues may be given written instructions instead of oral instructions.

- *Dates and places:* The IEP must state when services will begin, how often they will be provided, where they will be provided, and how long they will last.

- *Measuring progress:* The IEP must state how the child's progress will be measured and how parents will be informed of that progress.

Some common sensory IEP services include:

- The amount of time per week or month the child will spend in one-on-one therapy with an occupational therapist.

- The amount of time per week or month the parent will spend in consultation with an occupational therapist.

- The amount of time per week or month the child will spend in group therapy.

- Transportation services if needed.

Common sensory IEP accommodations include:

- Providing a calm place for the child to take a break when he or she feels overstimulated.

- Providing movement breaks during the school day or sensory activities prior to times when the child will need to focus.

- Using a weighted lap pad, vest, or neck pad to help achieve calm and focus.

- Using fidgeting toys and/or items to chew to help achieve calm and focus.

- Covering fluorescent lighting with a light-diffusing shade to minimize the effect of flickering. Some children can actually see the flickering of fluorescent lights. This can lead to sleepiness, headaches, nausea, and/or distraction from learning. This becomes more pronounced as a bulb begins to wear out, so regular maintenance should also be a priority.

- Providing warnings ahead of time about loud noises or potentially overstimulating experiences, such as fire drills.

- Allowing the child to use headphones in noisy areas, such as the gym, or to help the child concentrate.

- Minimizing visual clutter, which can distract students from instruction. An easy way to accommodate this IEP goal is to make sure the teacher provides instruction in front of a blank dry-erase board and uses curtains to cover shelves or rarely used classroom materials.

- Allowing for self-soothing behaviors, such as chewing on a chewy necklace or gum, holding onto a hand-fidget object, rocking, or kicking against an exercise band placed across the legs of a student's chair.

- Providing extra time for transitions.

- Providing special seating for the child—for example, sitting in the front of the class, at the back of the class, or away from doors and windows, which could provide visual or auditory distractions.

- Allowing the child to work standing up, sitting on a therapy ball, sitting on a wedge or T-stool, or sitting on a disk. These types of alternative seating can promote slight movement of core muscles and legs, which can help with concentration and focus—especially for a child who is fidgety.

- Allowing the child to stand in the front or the back of the line.

- Providing special pencil grips, wrist weights, or weighted writing utensils, which can help with gripping, controlling a pencil, and building fine-motor muscles.

- Allowing the child to eat in a quiet area if the cafeteria is too loud.

- Decreasing the amount of written work, focusing on quality versus quantity.

- Providing extra time for assignments to be completed.

- Providing graph paper to assist the child in working out math problems.

Note: If the child is receiving services through the local school district, the school district will assign a therapist to work with the child. There are many wonderful occupational therapists with strong backgrounds in sensory therapy that work in schools. However, not all occupational therapists are trained to work with children who have SPD. It is important to insist that the occupational therapist has experience with sensory-processing issues. If you believe that the therapist needs to have training in SPD to be able to work with your child, you can write that into the child's IEP.

Getting Services Privately

Finding an Occupational Therapist

If you are working outside of the school district or early intervention agency and need to find an occupational therapist for your child, start by putting together a list of all the occupational therapists in your area. A helpful place to find therapists that specialize in SPD is the Sensory Processing Disorder Foundation's Web site, the SPD Network *(www.spdfoundation.net)*. The SPD network has a directory of occupational therapists, physical therapists, speech-language pathologists, and others who specialize in children with sensory issues. For Canadians, *OTWorks.ca* has a section called "OT Finder" that can help locate professionals in your area. Another great place to find out about knowledgeable professionals is through a local parent support group for special-needs kids.

Interview the Therapist

Once you have compiled a list of potential therapists, call to schedule a time to interview him or her. When asking your questions, pay attention to the personality of the therapist. Is he or she patient? Does she answer your questions clearly? Do you feel comfortable with him?

Questions to ask a prospective therapist:

- Are you certified by the National Board of Certification in Occupational Therapy?
- Are your staff members trained and experienced in working with children who have SPD?
- How successful has your program been for other children?
- How is progress measured?
- How much individual attention will my child receive?
- Is parent training and consultation an important part of the program?
- Will the program prepare me to continue the therapy at home?

If, after talking with the therapist, you are interested in working with him or her, ask for references. Call other families who are working with her and see how their experience has been. Is she easy to work with? Are the children in other families progressing? Do their children enjoy the program? Would they recommend her?

Observe the Facility

Once you find an occupational therapist you're interested in working with, it's time to observe him or her in action. Pay attention to the facility—does it have well-maintained equipment that can provide a variety of sensory and movement opportunities? Are the therapists using play and encouragement to motivate children to actively participate in therapy? Are the children crying or resisting therapy? Is the therapy one on one, in a group setting, or a little of both? After you've observed therapy sessions in progress, is the therapist able to answer questions in an easy-to-understand manner?

Starting Therapy

The child has received a diagnosis, and a therapist has been assigned to work with him: It's time for therapy to begin! Remember, the goal of sensory therapy is to challenge a child's nervous system, but not to the point of overwhelming him. Before starting therapy, a good therapist will review all of the child's evaluation results.

On the basis of the evaluation findings and observations, the therapist will customize each session to meet the child's needs. Experienced therapists try to set up the environment to allow the child to guide the sessions. When a child is actively exploring this type of environment, it stimulates his nervous system, allowing him to interpret sensory information more appropriately. A good therapist will pay attention to what the child enjoys and his interests and will work these components into each therapy session. An inviting environment with fun, engaging, and interesting choices often inspires the child to explore it and participate.

During each session, the therapist will closely monitor the child. She will look for signs of overstimulation and monitor how engaged the child is in each activity. She will work to carefully challenge the child with appropriate sensory stimulation, without overwhelming him. The best therapists often look like they are just playing with the child. Therapists will usually create a *sensory diet* to address the child's needs, suggesting activities and sensory strategies to help the child be successful throughout the day.

What Is a Sensory Diet?

A sensory diet is a schedule of sensory exercises an occupational therapist will suggest for the child to do throughout the day. These activities are designed to help a child function well during the day and learn to properly interpret his or her environment. Let's think about diets for a minute—if a person receives a diagnosis of heart disease, a doctor will prescribe a heart-healthy diet. This could be a diet low in fat, which contains lots of fruits and vegetables, and includes an exercise program. Similarly, an occupational therapist may prescribe a healthy sensory diet. It may be rich in tactile experiences, such as a brushing program, as well as certain physical activities the child should do throughout the day to help him stay calm or become more alert when needed.

Speaking of diets, have you ever failed to follow a diet? If you have, chances are it was because you were not satisfied. You walked around feeling hungry or deprived of something you craved. A child who is a sensory seeker or craver may feel this way. He is walking around hungry for certain kinds of sensory stimulation. It is our job to give him what he needs. We need to provide a variety of appropriate sensory activities to meet his particular needs. Conversely, the overresponsive child or one with sensory-based motor disorder may restrict certain types of sensory stimulation to the extent that she becomes malnourished. In this case, it is our job to provide her with a balanced diet of sensory experiences.

A close working relationship with a child's therapist is essential to sensory therapy. A child's therapist will have good ideas for adapting an activity or challenging a child appropriately. He or she will be aware of behaviors and signs of overstimulation to watch out for. She can evaluate progress and provide suggestions to enable a child to keep progressing. Always consult a child's therapist before trying new activities or whenever questions arise. Please remember that not all of the activities in this book are appropriate for every child.

Follow Your Child's Lead!

Children frequently come up with innovative and fun extensions for activities. When they are allowed to explore new ideas, create new scenarios, and take on new roles, they stay active and interested in the activity. As long as they stay safe and their play doesn't enhance or encourage unhealthy behaviors—*anything goes!*

Watch Out for Overstimulation!

Children can become fatigued or overstimulated during sensory therapy. It may be time to take a break if you notice that the child:

- Turns away from the activity.
- Avoids looking at you.

- Closes her eyes.

- Covers her ears.

- Sneezes, yawns, or has the hiccups.

- Acts out or becomes defiant.

- Becomes overly anxious, fearful, or tired.

- Whines, cries, or asks to stop.

Life Is a Series of Small Steps

I have many dear friends that began sensory therapy with their children at the time I began working with my son. Our children are more confident, relaxed, and less fearful, and interpreting their environment much better today than when we first started. Sensory therapy also provided lots of positive interaction with our children along the way! I hope these activities will be fun and helpful to you, as well. Best wishes on your journey ahead!

CHAPTER 2

TACTILE ACTIVITIES

The house was too quiet. I called out for my son, but heard only wild laughter. I followed the laughter down the hall to the living room, turned a corner, and almost passed out. My son was lying on the coffee table, swimming in maple syrup! He looked at me, smiled, and did the breaststroke. I watched in horror as tiny droplets of maple syrup dripped off the table onto the carpet. The next couple of hours were a blur of showering, scrubbing, and carpet cleaning. I wanted to put locks on my refrigerator and cabinets!

Later that week, I met with my son's occupational therapist. I shared my syrup experience and my frustration. She explained that my son was not disobedient or out of control; his body was directing him to what he needed—lots of tactile stimulation! Once I started providing lots of alternative tactile activities, these sorts of messy surprises became a thing of the past. This chapter contains many of our favorites.

Shaving Cream Fun

A tip for easy cleanup—do these activities in the bathtub! Shaving cream is water soluble and will wash right off. You may want to use an unscented type for sensitive skin, since some children respond to strong smells. Try this activity in the evening, before bath time. You can also enjoy this activity on a table by using a cookie sheet. I keep a special activity towel nearby for all of our messy fun. If you are doing this activity in the classroom, use masking tape to section off areas of the table for each student. This is a great activity if your table is stained or has dried paint on it, as the shaving cream cleans the table nicely.

What you will need:

- [ ] plain shaving cream
- [ ] food coloring
- [ ] small plastic containers
- [ ] large cookie sheet
- [ ] towel

Optional items:

- [ ] toy cars, dinosaurs, or other plastic animals
- [ ] sponges, Q-tips, paintbrushes, or cotton balls

Begin by spreading a baseball-sized amount of shaving cream on the side of the bathtub or on a cookie sheet. Allow the child to finger-paint with the shaving cream.

You may suggest toe-painting, as well.

Caution: This can be very slippery!

Make sure the child is sitting down and her body has plenty of support, so she doesn't fall. You may want to support her by holding her under the arms. Allow her to lean back and paint with her feet. You can also easily toe-paint outside. Place a cookie sheet with shaving cream on some grass. Have the child sit next to it, either on the grass or in a chair for support, as she paints with her toes. When it's time to clean up, rinse off her feet with a hose and dry with your activity towel.

Extend It!

Color Mixing

Fill two small plastic containers with baseball-sized amounts of shaving cream. Add two drops of food coloring to each container and mix them up. Primary colors (red, yellow, and blue) work best. Place the colors next to each other and encourage the child to mix them and make a new color.

Shaving-Cream Paints

Fill a couple of small plastic containers with baseball-sized amounts of shaving cream. Add two drops of food coloring to each container, and mix them up. The child can finger-paint with the colors or paint with paintbrushes, Q-tips, cotton balls, or sponges.

Making Tracks

Plastic dinosaurs, toy animals, action figures, or toy cars can make tracks through the shaving cream.

 Rubbings

Be sure to spread some newspapers or garbage bags over the table before starting this activity—especially if your crayons are not washable! To make this activity even easier, use washable crayons.

What you will need:

- ☐ crayons
- ☐ chalk
- ☐ inexpensive paper
- ☐ empty cereal boxes

Optional items:

- ☐ coins, embossed cards, silverware handles, leaves, other textured items

Cut an empty cereal box into various small shapes. Place them under a sheet of paper, and let the child rub chalk or crayons over the paper until he sees the imprints of the shapes. You can also use other flat objects underneath, such as coins, embossed cards, and silverware handles.

Extend It!

Nature Walk

Go outside with paper and chalk. Let the child find things to use for rubbing, such as leaves, flowers, small twigs, tire tread, or tree bark. There are so many interesting things to touch and feel outdoors—the sky is the limit!

Paper Leaves

Gather several leaves from outside. Place them under a sheet of paper and encourage the child to rub the paper with a crayon to make the imprints show through. Cut out the colored leaves.

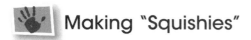 ## Making "Squishies"

These simple, homemade "squishies" can be very calming and last quite a long time. If your child is aggressive with her squeezing, use two balloons.

What you will need:

- [ ] sand, salt, rice, birdseed, or flour
- [ ] funnel (or a paper plate folded into a funnel shape)
- [ ] balloons (medium-sized)
- [ ] pencil or small spoon

Optional items:

- [ ] tempura paint (or other "kid paint"), dish soap, shallow bowl, paper bag, or butcher paper

With a funnel, fill each balloon with a cup of one or two grainy ingredients. If you are having trouble filling the balloons, use a pencil or small spoon to gently push the material in. Tie the balloons shut, making sure you have squeezed out any extra air. Give it to your child and let her squeeze away!

Extend It!

Squishy Painting

Mix one to two tablespoons of tempura paint with a squirt of dish soap in a shallow bowl. This will keep the paint from splattering and make cleanup much easier. If you don't have tempura paint, almost any kind of "kid paint" will work—I've even used shaving-cream paint! Use the paint to make wrapping paper by dipping the "squishy" you made into the paint and stamping a paper bag or a sheet of butcher paper.

Squishy Box

Make several types of squishies. Fill a variety of balloons with sand, flour, salt, rice, beans, birdseed, and so on. Put the squishies in a shoebox, and you have your own squishy box—a variety for the child to choose from!

Pass the Squishy

This game was inspired by the old game, "Hot Potato." Sing the song below to the tune of "London Bridge." Use the speed of your singing to control the speed of the game. As the song is sung slowly, pass the squishy slowly. As you speed up your singing, the pace of the game should also increase.

Pass the squishy, pass it now, pass it now, pass it now.
Pass the squishy, pass it now, pass it now.

Variations

- Pass it fast
- Pass it slow
- Pass it high
- Pass it low

 Shampoo Finger Paints

Do this in the bathtub for easy cleanup. It's a perfect activity to do in the evening, before bath time. You can also do it on a large cookie sheet or on the shiny side of freezer paper! The butcher has always been kind enough to give me extra paper when I ask him.

What you will need:

- ☐ white or colorless shampoo
- ☐ food coloring
- ☐ small plastic cups or muffin tins
- ☐ large cookie sheet or freezer paper
- ☐ towel

Optional items:

- ☐ salt or sawdust
- ☐ cotton balls, Q-tips, sponges, paintbrushes, combs, or Popsicle sticks
- ☐ toy cars, dinosaurs, or other small plastic animals

Pour small amounts of shampoo, about the size of a quarter each, into little cups. Add two drops of food coloring, different colors in each cup, and mix them up. Make two or three colors. Allow the child to finger-paint on the cookie sheet, freezer paper, or sides of the bathtub. For texture, add salt or sawdust to the paint. (If you're using sawdust, don't do this activity in the bathtub!)

Extend It!

More Painting Fun

Encourage the child to paint with paintbrushes, combs, Popsicle sticks, Q-tips, cotton balls, or sponges.

Sponge Prints

Cut a few sponges into simple shapes. Allow the child to make prints by dipping them into the paint.

Lather Up

Give the child wet sponges. Let him rub the paint back and forth to make thick, foamy lather. Once it's lathered up, he can finger-paint in it some more. For more fun, add some toy cars, dinosaurs, or animals and let him make tracks in the lather.

This activity also can be done with gel, apricot facial scrub, or cold cream. For a child who is overresponsive to smells, use unscented products.

 # Hair-Gel Bags

These squishy bags are very easy to create and will last quite a while (if they are not bitten!). If your child is particularly aggressive, use two bags.

What you will need:

- ☐ hair gel
- ☐ sparkly items (glitter or sequins)
- ☐ Ziploc sandwich bags
- ☐ duct tape

Optional items:

- ☐ grocery bag or large sheet of paper
- ☐ beads

Open a Ziploc sandwich bag, and squirt about ¼ cup of hair gel inside. Place a bit of glitter or a few sequins inside the bag, as well. Close the bag securely, seal it with duct tape at the zipper end, and let the child squish the contents around.

Extend It!

Tic-Tac-Toe

Make 10 hair-gel bags, and add two different colors of food coloring so you've got five bags with each color (for example, five red bags and five blue). Draw a large Tic-Tac-Toe grid on a piece of paper or grocery bag and play Tic-Tac-Toe. Instead of Xs and Os, one person uses hair-gel bags of one color, and the other participant uses the second color. Add beads to the bags for more texture!

Tracing Fun

Place a simple maze or design under the hair-gel bag. Have the child trace her way through the maze or trace the design through the bag.

 ## Edible Finger Paint

For easy cleanup, place some newspapers over a table. Allow the child to finger-paint on a clean cookie sheet instead of using paper.

What you will need:

- ☐ prepared vanilla pudding or plain yogurt
- ☐ food coloring
- ☐ muffin tin
- ☐ cookie sheet
- ☐ newspaper

Put a large spoonful of pudding or yogurt into each cup of a muffin tin. Add one or two drops of food coloring to each tin and mix well. Allow the child to finger-paint on a cookie sheet. These paints dry shiny and have texture. After the child is done, he can eat what's left or lick the picture he made!

 # Spaghetti Fun

These activities are very silly.

What you will need:

- ☐ cooked spaghetti
- ☐ small balls
- ☐ finger paint or other "kid paint"
- ☐ pie tins
- ☐ paper or large cookie sheet
- ☐ large pot of water

Spaghetti Painting

Cook some spaghetti with oil in the water to keep it from sticking. Have the child dip the spaghetti into pie tins of paint. Let her paint with the spaghetti on paper or a large cookie sheet. If using her hands is too challenging at first, suggest using tongs.

Spaghetti and Meatballs

Cook some spaghetti and put it in a large pot of cool water. Add some small rubber balls to the pot. Place the pot in the kitchen sink and let the child play with the spaghetti and "meatballs." This activity is also nice to do outside during recess.

Spaghetti Writing

Cook some spaghetti with oil in the water to keep it from sticking. Trace letters, numbers, or the child's name on a piece of paper. Let him outline the letters with spaghetti.

 Play Dough

There are several ways to have fun with play dough, while creating less mess. If you have a small plastic swimming pool, let your child play with the play dough inside it. If you're sitting at a table, set a large rubber mat under a cookie sheet so it will not slide around, and let the child play with the play dough there. Spread an inexpensive vinyl tablecloth under the child's chair. When he is done playing, shake out and fold up the tablecloth, and throw away the play dough.

Note: If play dough gets on your carpet, do not get it wet. This will make it much more difficult to clean. Let it dry, break it apart, and vacuum it up.

Here are two recipes to make your own play dough—cooked and uncooked!

Cooked Play Dough Recipe

What you will need:

- ☐ 1½ cups flour
- ☐ ¾ cup salt
- ☐ 3 tablespoons cream of tartar
- ☐ 1½ cups water
- ☐ 3 tablespoons oil
- ☐ food coloring
- ☐ medium bowl
- ☐ large bowl
- ☐ 9 x 9-inch pan
- ☐ resealable bags or containers

Mix the dry ingredients together in a medium-sized bowl. In a large bowl, combine the liquid ingredients, then stir in the dry ones. Bake in a 9 x 9-inch pan at 350°F for 7 to 10 minutes. Cool and knead. Store in a resealable bag or in yogurt cups to keep it fresh.

Uncooked Play Dough Recipe

What you will need:

- ☐ 2 cups flour
- ☐ 1 cup salt
- ☐ 1 cup warm water
- ☐ food coloring
- ☐ large bowl
- ☐ resealable bags or containers

Optional items:

- ☐ cookie cutters and plastic kitchen utensils
- ☐ beans, beads, or rice
- ☐ latex or vinyl glove

Note: Many people are allergic to latex. If allergies are a concern, use a vinyl or other nonlatex glove.

In a large bowl, mix the food coloring and water together, then add the dry ingredients. Knead the dough until it is well blended. If your child wants to, let her knead the dough. For something different, pour the ingredients into a resealable bag and close it tight, making sure to get all of the air out. Give the bag to the child and let her knead the ingredients until they are blended. Provide cookie cutters and plastic kitchen utensils and let her play. Store dough in resealable bags or containers.

Extend It!

Color Mixing

Take a ball of yellow dough and a ball of blue, and mix them together to make green.

Bumpy Dough

Mix beans or beads into the play dough.

Squishy Gloves

Put play dough (or rice) into a latex glove. Tie the top and let your child squish!

 **Blubber**

A child can play with blubber just like play dough. It has a bouncy, rubbery, stretchy feel.

Caution: If blubber dries on carpet, it is very difficult to remove. Also, don't ever put blubber or other goopy substances down the drain. They may clog it! Always throw blubber away in the trash.

At the table, set a large cookie sheet on a rubber mat, so it will not slide around. Spread an inexpensive vinyl tablecloth under the child's chair. After the activity, fold the tablecloth and *throw out the leftover blubber.* Blubber can be stored in a sealed container for several weeks.

What you will need:

- ☐ 1 teaspoon 20 Mule Team Borax natural laundry booster
- ☐ 1 cup water
- ☐ 4 ounces white glue
- ☐ 4 ounces water
- ☐ 7–10 drops of food coloring
- ☐ 2 bowls
- ☐ plastic knives, cookie cutters, mini rolling pins

In one bowl, mix the Borax with 1 cup of warm water until it dissolves. In a second bowl, mix the glue with 4 ounces of water and food coloring. Slowly pour the glue mixture into the Borax and water while stirring. Roll the blubber in the water mixture three or four times. Pull out the blubber and rinse it off in cold water. Provide plastic knives, cookie cutters, and mini rolling pins and let the child cut, flatten, and try to shape the blubber.

Add more or less water to the glue to change the consistency of the blubber. For this mixture, a little food coloring goes a long way! Too much coloring can transfer to the child's hands or the table.

Beans, Rice, and Birdseed Fun

This is a very messy activity. The trick to easier cleanup is to do it in the bathtub or in a small plastic swimming pool. Make sure the drain in the tub is plugged and the tub or swimming pool is dry. When finished, just sweep up the beans and put them into a bin for reuse. Two-gallon stackable containers work well for storage.

What you will need:

- ☐ beans, rice, birdseed, dry macaroni, or oatmeal
- ☐ large plastic bin or large pot
- ☐ sand toys

Optional items:

- ☐ cooking utensils, plastic cups, funnels
- ☐ small plastic animals or toy cars

Pour any combination of beans, rice, birdseed, or other dry, grainy substances into a large plastic bin or pot (placed in the bathtub or plastic swimming pool). Let the child play in it.

Extend It!

Cooking

Introduce cooking utensils, plastic cups, spoons, and funnels and encourage the child to pretend to cook. He can measure ingredients, stir them, add new ingredients, and so on.

Hide and Seek

Hide small plastic animals, cars, and trains and let the child find them.

 Pud

Pud feels hard when grabbed, yet it will turn into a liquid when you let go.

This is a messy activity. If the pud is colored with food coloring, it will come off on the child's hands. However, if you have a child who really craves tactile stimulation, it's great. Set the container of pud on top of a cookie sheet, newspaper, or grocery bag for easy cleanup.

What you will need:

- ☐ 1 cup cornstarch
- ☐ 1 cup water
- ☐ food coloring

Optional items:

- ☐ plastic dinosaurs or small plastic airplanes

Mix the water and a couple of drops of food coloring together in a pot or 2-quart container.

Note: If your container is plastic, the food coloring may stain it!

Slowly add the cornstarch and wait a couple of minutes. Let your child play in the "pud."

Extend It!

Dinosaur Fun

Add black or brown food coloring (or mix various colors for this effect) to make a tar pit. Add small plastic dinosaurs and let them get stuck. Make tracks and watch them disappear. Have the child "excavate" the tar pit by digging up the dinosaurs.

Flying Fun

Color the pud blue. Add some small plastic airplanes and let the child fly them in and out of the pud.

 ## Paint Dough

This paint is three dimensional and glossy when dry. The paint stays contained, so this activity is not too messy. Simply cover a table with a vinyl tablecloth or some newspaper.

What you will need:

- ☐ ¼ cup flour
- ☐ ¼ cup salt
- ☐ ¼ cup water
- ☐ Ziploc bags or squeeze bottles
- ☐ food coloring
- ☐ paper or cookie sheet
- ☐ towel
- ☐ vinyl tablecloth or newspaper

Optional items:

- ☐ muffin tin
- ☐ sponges, cotton balls, paintbrushes
- ☐ cardboard
- ☐ beans, grains, or beads

Pour the dry ingredients into a Ziploc bag. You can also use plastic squeeze bottles (such as empty ketchup or mustard bottles). Then mix the water and food coloring together and add them to the dry ingredients. Seal the baggie, making sure there is no air in the bag. Give the child the bag and let her squish it until the ingredients are mixed together, or let her shake the bottle until the ingredients are combined. Cut a hole in the corner of the baggie and allow the child to squeeze the paint dough out onto some paper or a cookie sheet.

Extend It!

Paint with the Paint Dough

Fill muffin tins with several colors of paint dough. Allow the child to paint by using sponges, cotton balls, paintbrushes, or her fingers.

Name Board

Write a child's name on a piece of cardboard. Encourage her to cover the letters with paint dough. Decorate the dough with beans, grains, or beads.

"NO-COOK" COOKING

FUN, EASY, AND EDIBLE!

 ## Peanut Butter Cookie Recipe

Make and eat these in 5 minutes!

What you will need:

- ☐ 1 tablespoon peanut butter
- ☐ 1 tablespoon nonfat milk
- ☐ 1 graham cracker
- ☐ resealable sandwich bags
- ☐ cake pan

Optional items:

- ☐ coconut or sprinkles

Place a graham cracker inside a cake pan, and have the child use his fingers to crumble it into fine pieces. Place the crumbs into a sandwich bag. Add the peanut butter and nonfat milk to the bag. Seal the bag, making sure all of the air is out. Have the child knead the bag until the ingredients are mixed. Open the bag, take out the dough, roll it into small balls, and eat. Roll the cookies in sprinkles or coconut for an added treat!

 Ant Farm

What you will need:

- ☐ graham crackers
- ☐ chocolate sprinkles
- ☐ resealable sandwich bags
- ☐ cake pan

Optional items:

- ☐ raisins or gummy worms

Place a graham cracker inside a cake pan and have the child use her fingers to crumble it into fine pieces. Place the crumbs into a sandwich bag. Give the child a shaker with chocolate sprinkles and let her sprinkle in the "ants." Close the bag and shake it up. Let the child eat the "ant farm," using her fingers or a small spoon. For variety, use raisins or gummy worms instead of sprinkles.

 # Watermelon Slushie

What you will need:

- ☐ seedless watermelon
- ☐ resealable sandwich bag
- ☐ straw
- ☐ spoon
- ☐ plastic knife

Give the child a slice of melon (without the rind) and a plastic knife. Let the child cut the melon into small cubes and place them into a sandwich bag. Seal the bag, and have the child squish the melon to make juice. Afterward, open a corner of the bag and insert a straw. Let the child drink the juice. Give him a spoon to eat the leftover pulp.

Easy Doughnut Recipe

What you will need:

- ☐ electric skillet or shallow pan
- ☐ oil
- ☐ cookie sheet
- ☐ flour
- ☐ canned biscuits
- ☐ resealable sandwich bag
- ☐ cinnamon
- ☐ confectioner's sugar

Optional items:

- ☐ cocoa powder

Heat the oil in an electric skillet. Cover a cookie sheet with a small amount of flour and place a biscuit on the flour coating. Put the cookie sheet on the table in front of the child. Allow the child to roll the dough into a long line. Then have her bring both ends together to make a doughnut. Cook the doughnut in the skillet until golden brown. Be careful—hot oil burns! When the doughnut has cooled, give the child a baggie with confectioner's sugar and cinnamon in it, and have her shake her doughnut in the baggie to coat it.

Extend It!

Fried Worms

Have the child roll the dough into a long line to make a "worm." Cook the worm in the heated oil. When it has cooled, give the child a baggie with a scoop of cocoa in it and let him cover the worm with "dirt."

 ## Make a Salad

What you will need:

- ☐ lettuce
- ☐ vegetables

Making salad is a great tactile activity. Additionally, when children are involved in preparing something, they are more likely to eat it! Have the child wash the lettuce, break it into small pieces, and place it in a bowl. Next, let the child practice cutting a variety of vegetables. Depending on the age of the child, you can use a plastic knife for tomatoes or a sharper knife for something like carrots or celery. Remember to always supervise kids when using knives!

 ## Banana Bugs

What you will need:

- ☐ bananas
- ☐ pretzel sticks
- ☐ plastic knife

Let the child peel the banana and then use the plastic knife to cut it in half. Poke the pretzels into the banana to make legs and antennae.

OTHER FOOD-RELATED ACTIVITIES

Play Hamburger

This activity feels great and can be very calming.

What you will need:

- ☐ couch cushions
- ☐ blanket

Lay a couch cushion on the floor. Have the child lie on the cushion, making sure her head is sticking out. Place another cushion on top of her.

Caution: Be sure the child's head is not between the cushions!

Kneel down by the child and slowly squish down on the top cushion by applying pressure. Go slowly, and ask the child if she wants you to keep pushing or if you should stop.

Extend It!

Add Condiments

While maintaining the pressure, extend the activity by moving the top cushion in circles to put on ketchup, rubbing back and forth to add mustard, or gently bouncing the top cushion to add pickles, lettuce, and tomatoes.

Hot Dog

Spread a blanket on the floor. Have the child lie down at the edge of the blanket, with his head sticking out over the edge of the blanket. Roll the child up tightly in the blanket.

Caution: Be sure the child is comfortable and that the child's head is not in the blanket.

Ask if he would like some ketchup. If so, rub across his body to add ketchup. Ask him if he would like relish, mustard, peanut butter, or whatever the two of you can think of. Change the way you rub his body for each condiment.

Body-Part Condiments

This time, *you* become the hamburger or the hot dog! Ask the child for some ketchup. Have her extend her arm, then grasp her arm firmly at the top near her shoulder and *squeeze downward,* pretending her arm is the ketchup bottle. Ask for mustard, and have the child use the other arm. Use a leg for mayonnaise, and so on.

Make a Bird Feeder

To cut down on the mess, use only ¼ inch of birdseed in a small cake pan and use a large cookie sheet.

What you will need:

- ☐ empty toilet paper roll or pinecone
- ☐ peanut butter
- ☐ birdseed
- ☐ yarn or string
- ☐ butter knife
- ☐ towel

Optional items:

- ☐ carrot, large pretzel, or celery stick
- ☐ cream cheese or frosting
- ☐ coconut, sprinkles, or crushed graham crackers

On a paper plate, place an empty toilet paper roll or a pinecone, a butter knife, and a small scoop of peanut butter. Set the paper plate on a cookie sheet at the table. Have the child cover the toilet paper roll or pinecone with peanut butter, then roll it in birdseed. To hang the birdfeeder, punch a hole at one end and tie a loop of string or yarn through the hole to make a hanger.

Extend It!

My Feeder

Give the child a carrot, large pretzel, or stick of celery to cover in peanut butter, cream cheese, or frosting. Let him roll it in coconut, sprinkles, or crushed graham crackers. Then let him eat it!

FUN FEELY STUFF

 String Designs

When dry, these designs can be very pretty if they're hung from string or taped to a window.

What you will need:

- ☐ yarn
- ☐ ¼ cup white glue
- ☐ ¼ cup water
- ☐ wax paper or aluminum foil
- ☐ cookie sheet
- ☐ wide, shallow bowl
- ☐ towel

Optional items:

- ☐ clothespin
- ☐ marker
- ☐ paper
- ☐ balloon, medium-sized

Use a wide, shallow bowl to mix the water and glue. Use a cookie sheet lined with aluminum foil or wax paper as a work surface. Also have a towel handy.

Cut several pieces of yarn to lengths of 6-12 inches. Have the child dip the yarn in the glue, then run her fingers down the yarn to squeeze off the excess. Encourage the child to make designs by placing the string on wax paper or aluminum foil. If touching the yarn is too challenging at first, allow her to use a clothespin to dip and place the yarn.

Extend It!

Learn Your Letters

With a marker, write letters, numbers, or the child's name on a piece of paper. Ask the child to trace the design with the yarn.

Ornaments

Use holiday yarn. Draw a 6 x 6-inch box on the wax paper. Have the child make overlapping shapes with the yarn inside the box. Let the yarn dry, peel the design off the paper, and loop some more yarn through the top of the design to hang it for the holidays!

Bird in a Cage

Blow up a medium-sized balloon and tie it shut. Wet the yarn with the glue mixture and wrap it around the balloon until it resembles a cage. Let the yarn dry, pop the balloon, and pull out the pieces. Cut out a paper "bird" and punch a small hole in the top of the bird by using a pencil. Hang the bird inside the cage with string. You can hang the cage in a child's bedroom as a pretend "pet," or liven up the windows of the classroom with colorful birds and cages. For this to work well, use a mixture of ⅔ cup glue and ⅓ cup water.

Eggshell Pictures

What you will need:

- heavy paper or cardboard
- newspaper
- white glue
- small paintbrush
- food coloring
- vinegar
- hot water
- cups
- cracked eggshells
- large cookie sheet
- margarine tub or other disposable plastic bowl with lid

To Dye the Eggshells

Remember to do this activity on a large cookie sheet for easy cleanup! Combine ½ cup of hot water and 1 teaspoon of vinegar, and add 20 drops of food coloring. Make two or three colors by following this procedure. Place the eggshells in the colored water, and let them soak for about 5 minutes. Take the eggshells out and place them on newspaper. Let them dry for about 10 minutes. When dry, crumble the eggshells into even smaller pieces.

To Make the Eggshell Art

Draw an oval on some cardboard and have the child "paint" it with glue. To keep the glue from getting messy, make a glue tub. Cut a ½-inch hole in the top of a small plastic margarine tub. Fill the tub with ½ inch of glue and put on the lid. Give the child a small paintbrush and allow him to dip the brush into the tub through the hole. When the glue has been painted on, then have the child decorate the "egg" with the crushed shells. This is a great activity to do right after Easter!

Extend It!

Fun Pictures

Decorate simple pictures like butterflies, make circles to decorate as planets, or draw flowers to cover in the colored eggshell bits.

 Soapy Fun

Filling a sink full of bubbles is a simple activity that's a lot of fun. An inexpensive hand-cranked eggbeater (bought at the store for 5 dollars!) was well worth the investment for this activity.

What you will need:

- ☐ towel
- ☐ water
- ☐ dish soap or bubble bath
- ☐ eggbeater, whisk, sponges, turkey baster, funnel, or plastic cups

Optional items:

- ☐ plastic baby doll
- ☐ handkerchiefs, socks, or potholders
- ☐ ice cubes

Plug the kitchen sink, pour in some soap, and add some water. Beat or whisk the water to create a fair amount of bubbles. Pour in the kitchen utensils and let the child have fun. Place a towel on the floor, so it won't get too slippery. If your child is splashing a lot of water, put less in the sink, or do the activity in the bathtub.

To do this activity in the bathtub, place a large plastic bin filled with soapy water in the bathtub. Have the child sit next to the bin on a towel.

Caution: This activity can be very slippery.

Extend It!

Wash the Baby

Give the child a washcloth and a plastic baby doll and let her wash the baby.

Laundry

Give the child several small items with different textures, such as handkerchiefs, socks, or potholders, and let her wash them, wring them out, and hang them to dry.

Arctic Fun

Instead of soap, put ice cubes in the water for some chilly fun. Freeze a large piece of ice to put in the water as an iceberg.

Tissue Paper Fun

Caution: The ink from tissue paper can stain clothes or hands.

What you will need:

- [ ] white glue
- [ ] water
- [ ] paper cup or glue tub
- [ ] tissue paper
- [ ] construction paper
- [ ] paintbrush
- [ ] cookie sheet
- [ ] newspaper

Optional items:

- [ ] large plastic lid

Mix about 2 tablespoons of glue with 1 tablespoon of water in a paper cup or a glue tub. (To make a glue tub, cut a ½-inch hole in the top of a small plastic margarine tub. Fill the tub with ½ inch of glue and put on the lid. Give the child a small paintbrush and allow him to dip the brush into the tub through the hole.)

Cover a cookie sheet with newspaper. Place the cup of glue or the glue tub on the cookie sheet with a piece of construction paper. Give the child several sheets of tissue paper to rip into pieces. Then have the child paint some glue onto the construction paper and press the tissue paper pieces on it to decorate it. She may want to crumple the paper or wad it into small balls, which is fine, too.

Extend It!

Sun Catcher

For this activity, you will also need a large plastic lid. Give the child a couple of differently colored sheets of tissue and let him rip them into several pieces. Have the child paint the lid with glue. Then encourage him to decorate the lid with the torn tissue paper. Let the lid dry for a couple of days. When it is completely dry, peel the sun catcher out of the lid. Punch a hole in the top, and tie a ribbon through it. Hang it in the window. Remember to save the lid for another time! These look wonderful when hung in the classroom windows.

 Crinkle Bag

What you will need:

- ☐ old pillowcase, large garbage bag, or grocery bag
- ☐ fall leaves or crumpled newspapers
- ☐ string

Fill an old pillowcase, large garbage bag, or plastic grocery bag with fallen leaves or newspapers and tie it shut. Let your child squeeze the bag, sit on it, or jump on it.

 Bubble Wrap

Never throw bubble wrap away! Save it and let your child walk across it barefoot, rub it with her hands, or pop the bubbles.

 Barefoot Fun

Take a barefoot walk. Walk on carpet and a tile floor, then go outside and walk on grass and cement and finish by walking in some mud. Hose off your feet outside and dry them with your activity towel.

You can also lay down clothing with different textures, packaging material, bubble wrap, or anything else you have on hand that would be interesting to walk on.

 Sticky Bracelet

What you will need:

- ☐ masking tape or blue painter's tape
- ☐ things you find outside

For this activity, start by making a bracelet out of the tape—wrap a piece of tape around the child's wrist with the sticky side pointing out. Now go outside and find small things to stick to the bracelet. If this is a classroom project, at the end of the walk, cut the bracelets off everyone's hands and staple them to a bulletin board to make a nature collage.

 Thanksgiving Centerpiece

What you will need:

- ☐ small pumpkin
- ☐ fresh, dried, or silk flowers and leaves
- ☐ small plastic container or cup

Cut a hole in the top of a pumpkin. Allow the child to use a spoon to scoop out the pulp and seeds. Fill the plastic cup half full with pebbles, sand, or rice. Carefully place the plastic cup inside the pumpkin. Let the child arrange the flowers and leaves in the container.

Extend It!

Place the pulp and pumpkin seeds in a small bowl and let the child play with them.

Clean the seeds, let them dry, and place them in a bin to play with. Or, bake the seeds and eat them!

Papier-Mâché Buddies

What you will need:

- ☐ cardboard
- ☐ sharp scissors
- ☐ glue
- ☐ water
- ☐ shallow containers
- ☐ paper plates
- ☐ newspaper

Before you start this project, make sure to cover the work area with newspapers. With sharp scissors, cut a simple animal shape from the cardboard. Have the child tear the newspaper into 1 x 4-inch strips. Pour glue into a shallow container and dilute it with water. Let the child dip a single strip of newspaper into the glue mixture and then remove the excess glue by pulling the strip between his fingers. Place the strips on the cardboard animal so that the cardboard is completely covered. Continue applying strips until it has four or five layers of newspaper. Allow it to dry for a day or two. Once your animal is dry, decorate it by using markers or paint. These look wonderful when they're hanging in a classroom. For the holidays, cut out simple circles or stars and cover them with papier-mâché to make ornaments.

 Grape Stomp

What you will need:

- ☐ large plastic garbage bag
- ☐ grapes

This is an activity you'll want to do outside! Place a large garbage bag on the ground. Let the child pick grapes off the vine and put them on the bag. Have the child take her shoes and socks off, roll up her pants, and then stomp the grapes. Have a bucket of water or garden hose handy to clean her up at the end of this activity!

Extend It!

You can set a timer and see how many grapes someone can stomp in a minute. Place the grapes in a straight line on a mat, and have her stomp the grapes as she goes down the line.

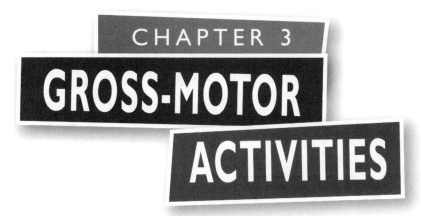

CHAPTER 3
GROSS-MOTOR ACTIVITIES

VESTIBULAR AND PROPRIOCEPTIVE GAMES

Most kids love tubes and slides. Many fast-food restaurants have capitalized on this by making indoor playgrounds filled with this equipment. On a rainy Saturday, these play places are often filled to capacity with children having a great time. However, for some children, this type of playground can seem like torture.

Tubes and slides—what's the big deal? They require accurate proprioceptive and vestibular information. For playgrounds to be fun, a child needs adequate balance and body awareness. If a child is not quite sure where her head is in relation to her surroundings, it's easy to bump it inside a tube. If a child's sense of balance is off, going down a slide can make her feel sick. Thus, for some children, tubes and slides can be scary or even nauseating! To develop the vestibular and proprioceptive senses, children need a safe, stress-free environment in which to practice moving their bodies.

FUN WITH BOXES

 **Swimming Box**

What you will need:

- ☐ large box
- ☐ packing peanuts
- ☐ sand toys

Fill a large box half full with packing peanuts. Place the child inside the box with a plastic pail and shovel, measuring spoons, cups, and bowls. Let the child explore.

Caution: Supervise this activity closely! Small children can choke on packing peanuts if not supervised properly. If you are worried your child will put the packing peanuts in his or her mouth, you can do this activity with puffed rice or wheat.

Mini Swimming Box

What you will need:

- ☐ small box or baby bathtub
- ☐ puffed cereal
- ☐ sand toys
- ☐ sheet or blanket

For a mini swimming box, use a small cardboard box or plastic baby bathtub. Fill it with puffed wheat or rice cereal and some sand toys. For easy cleanup, place the box in the middle of a sheet or blanket on the floor. When the child is done playing, fold the blanket and dump the cereal back into the cardboard box for use again later.

Extend It!

"Oh No, Where Did It Go?"

Put a large box in the middle of the room and let the child climb in. Say "Oh no, where did your head go?" Instruct the child to stick out his head. Repeat for hand, fingers, elbow, or leg. Have the child climb out of the box, lay it on its side, and call out body parts again.

Box Vehicles

Pretend a box is a vehicle. Have the child get into the box and give her a ride. Then, let her fill the box with her favorite toys and give them a ride, too.

Box Tunnels

Open two or more boxes on both ends and place them together to make a box tunnel. Encourage the child to crawl through it.

MOVEMENT GAMES

The following games are great for vestibular and proprioceptive input.

 ## Beanbag Robot

Give the child a beanbag, and explain that he is a robot and the beanbag is his battery. Have the child move around like a robot, balancing the beanbag on his head. When the beanbag falls, tell him to freeze because a robot can't move without its battery. Change the position of the beanbag to the shoulder or outstretched hand and repeat the game.

 ## Move Like an Animal

Think up various types of animals with your child, then move like them.

- For snakes, slither on the ground.
- For rabbits or kangaroos, jump up and down.
- For an elephant, clasp your hands together and swing them back and forth.
- For a cheetah, run in place as fast as you can.
- For a frog, crouch down and jump up!
- For a bird, flap your arms.
- For a penguin, keep both arms down stiff at your sides and waddle around.

Extend It!

Animal Charades

Make several cards, each with a different animal shown. Have the child choose a card and act out the animal while you try to guess what it is.

Animal Relays

Run like a bear on all fours. Move sideways on hands and knees like a crab. Squat low and hop like a bunny. Jump high like a kangaroo.

As a variation, become different bugs: a worm, butterfly, bee, spider, or grasshopper.

Clapping Game

Lead your child in this game.

Clap your hands.

Clap your hands fast, faster, fastest!

Clap your hands slow, slower, slowest.

Clap your hands high, high and fast, high and slow.

Clap your hands low, low and fast, low and slow.

Clap your hands big, bigger, biggest!

You can also flap your arms, stomp your feet, or clap with your feet for variety.

Follow the Leader

Play "follow the leader" with the child. Jump up and down, walk backwards, shake your body, spin in circles, push on the wall, hop on one foot, and so on. Switch places and let the child be the leader.

 Feather Game

What you will need:

- ☐ feathers
- ☐ paper plate

Give the child a feather. Place a plate 3 feet away. See if she can throw the feather so that it hits the plate. Vary the distance the child stands from the plate.

Extend It!

Have the child switch arms, bend down, and look between his legs to throw the feather, or have him turn around and throw it over his head.

 Feather Relay

What you will need:

- ☐ couch cushions or cones
- ☐ feather
- ☐ paper plate

Place several couch cushions or cones around the room. Place a feather on a paper plate and hand it to the child. See if she can make her way around the cushions without letting the feather fall off of the plate.

 ## Crazy Relay

What you will need:

☐ index cards

Write five silly instructions on separate index cards. For example—pat your head, jump up and down, or flap your arms like a chicken. Each child takes out an instruction card and performs the action; the next child takes out another card and performs the first action *plus* the action he just pulled out, and so on, until everyone has had a turn.

Note: If a child has a lot of issues with motor skills, let him go first and start with an easier action.

 ## Snowball Fight I

What you will need:

☐ a friend or two

☐ lots and lots of paper

☐ jump rope or blue painter's tape

Give the children a stack of paper and have them crinkle it into balls. Divide the room with a jump rope or make a line with blue painter's tape. Now it's time for a snowball fight! Let the children throw "snowballs" at each other. (You may be surprised by how much energy kids will use doing this!) When they're done, let the children clean up by throwing the paper into the trash or recycle bin.

MOVEMENT SONGS

Recite or sing at a pace comfortable for the child.

 Hammer Song

(To the tune of "Johnny Hammers with One Hammer")

> *I can work with one hammer, one hammer, one hammer.*
> (The child moves his arm up and down while making a fist.)

> *I can work with one hammer; I can work with two!*
> (The child moves both arms up and down while making fists.)

Continue the song in this pattern for these additional verses:

> *I can work with three!*
> (The child moves both arms and stomps with one leg.)

> *I can work with four!*
> (The child moves both arms and stomps with both legs.)

> *I can work with five!*
> (Now add the head nodding up and down.)

Then work backward:

> *I can work with five hammers, five hammers, five hammers.*

> *I can work with five hammers, I can work with four!*

 "Head and Shoulders"

Have the child touch the body parts to correspond with the song lyrics.

Head and shoulders, knees and toes, knees and toes,

Head and shoulders, knees and toes, knees and toes,

Eyes and ears, a mouth and a nose,

Head and shoulders, knees and toes, knees and toes!

"Little Red Wagon"

Bouncing up and down in my little red wagon,

Bouncing up and down in my little red wagon,

Bouncing up and down in my little red wagon,

Won't you be my darling!

Other verses:

Moving side to side in my little red wagon...
(Child sways left and right.)

Now I'm rolling off of my little red wagon...
(Child rolls on the ground.)

🎵 "Wheels on the Bus"

The wheels on the bus go round and round,

Round and round, round and round.

The wheels on the bus go round and round,

All through the town.
(Child rolls her arms around each other.)

Invent corresponding movements for each additional verse.

The doors on the bus go open and shut.

The driver on the bus says, "Move on back!"

The people on the bus go bumpity-bump.

The wipers on the bus go swish, swish, swish.

🎵 "Mulberry Bush"

Here we go 'round the mulberry bush,

The mulberry bush, the mulberry bush.

Here we go 'round the mulberry bush,

So early in the morning!
(The child walks around an object representing a mulberry bush.)

This is the way we wash our clothes,

Wash our clothes, wash our clothes.

This is the way we wash our clothes,

So early in the morning!
(The child pretends to dunk clothes into a bucket, scrub clothes on a washboard, and wring them out.)

Other verses:

This is the way we iron our clothes.

This is the way we scrub the floor.

This is the way we sweep the house.
(The child pretends to do the chore the verse describes.)

MOVING TO MUSIC

 ### Bounce to the Music

Place the child on your lap. Sing a song with a definite beat, and bounce the child on your knees. Vary the tempos and beats.

Caution: Do not bounce too hard, and do not perform this activity with very young children.

 ### Mirror Dance

Slow music works great for this activity. Put on some music and stand facing the child. Have the child copy your movements. Start with a simple movement, like waving one hand above your head, then wave both hands, and so on. Switch roles, and let the child make up moves to be mirrored.

 ### Freeze Dance

Play some music and have the child dance. When the music stops, he must freeze (stand still) until the music starts again.

 ## Musical Hugs

Play some music and dance with your child. When the music stops, give each other a big hug!

 ## Drum Your Body

Encourage the child to drum her body to the music. She can start by gently drumming on her head with her hands. Then move down the body, drumming shoulders, chest, stomach, thighs, and feet.

 ## Paper-Plate Dancing

Give the child a paper plate. Play different types of music and have the child keep the beat by tapping the plate on his head, tummy, knee, and elbow.

 ## Toilet-Paper Dancing

Give the child a length of toilet paper. This is her "streamer." Have her dance to music with her streamer. Instruct her to try not to let the streamer touch the ground. A scarf or paper streamers from the party supply store will also work.

BALLOON FUN

What you will need:

- ☐ balloons
- ☐ sticks for stirring paint (available at home-improvement and paint stores)
- ☐ paper plates

 ## Balloon Tennis

Blow up a balloon. Tape wooden paint stirrers to a couple of sturdy paper plates to make rackets. Toss the balloon in the air and play "balloon tennis" by tapping the balloon back and forth.

 ## Balloon Catch

Have the child throw a balloon up into the air and catch it with the paper plate.

 Balloon Dancing

Have the child dance while holding the balloon. Swing it side to side and up and down, or make circles with it to the music. Or, throw the balloon in the air and dance while trying to keep it from touching the floor.

 Balloon Jump

Hang a balloon from the ceiling or a tree branch. Let the child jump and hit the balloon with his hands or head. Vary the height of the balloon.

NEWSPAPER FUN

 ## Paper-Bag Faces

This is a very clean activity if the child decorates the bag with markers.

What you will need:

- ☐ small paper bag
- ☐ stapler
- ☐ markers
- ☐ newspaper

Optional items:

- ☐ yarn
- ☐ sequins
- ☐ buttons
- ☐ felt
- ☐ glue

Encourage the child to crumple up the newspaper and stuff the paper bag with it. When the bag is full, staple it shut to make a head. Let the child draw a face on the bag with markers. During October, you can use orange bags to make pumpkins, or white bags to make ghosts!

For a more elaborate version, decorate the bags with yarn, sequins, buttons, and felt shapes.

Paper Race

Cut large pieces of newspaper into the shape of feet. Put one foot in front of you and one in front of the child. Flap a piece of folded newspaper at the foot, so that you move it forward with the airflow. See who can "run" his or her foot to the other side of the room fastest. (Of course, my son always won...)

 ## Snowball Fight II

Give the child a stack of newspapers. Have him crumple them up into several snowballs. When all of the paper is wadded up, have a snowball fight!

 ## Ice Cream Recipe

There are two fun ways to make this great homemade treat. This is a clean activity, provided no one opens the bag! It takes 5 to 7 minutes to make; to pass the time, sing some songs.

What you will need:

- ☐ 1 cup whole milk
- ☐ 3 tablespoons sugar
- ☐ 1 teaspoon vanilla
- ☐ ¼ cup rock salt
- ☐ ice (crushed ice works best but is not necessary.)
- ☐ 1 pint-sized resealable plastic bag
- ☐ 1 gallon-sized resealable plastic bag or two coffee cans with lids, one can larger than the other

Plastic Bag Method

Combine the milk, sugar, and vanilla. Pour the mixture into a pint-sized bag and seal. Fill a gallon-sized plastic bag half full of ice and pour in the rock salt. Place the smaller bag of the milk mixture into the larger bag of ice, and seal the larger bag. Encourage the child to shake the bag for 5 to 7 minutes. If the bag gets a hole and starts to leak, simply place it inside another resealable bag. When the ice cream is set, take the smaller bag out and snip off one of the corners. Let the child squeeze the ice cream into a bowl and eat it!

Coffee Can Method

Combine the milk, sugar, and vanilla in the smaller coffee can and put the lid on. Put the smaller can into the larger can. Fill the space between the two cans with ice and rock salt. Put the lid on the larger can. Roll the can back and forth between you and the child for 5 to 7 minutes, until the ice cream is set. If you have several children, you can sit in a circle and take turns rolling the can to each other!

 ## Making Pudding

What you will need:

- ☐ cold milk
- ☐ instant pudding mix
- ☐ empty yogurt cup and lid
- ☐ tape
- ☐ spoon

Fill a clean yogurt cup half full of cold milk and a teaspoon of instant pudding. Put the cover on the cup, tape it shut, and let the child shake it for a minute or two. Take the lid off the container and give her a spoon for an instant treat. You can also use baby-food jars instead of yogurt cups.

 ## Making Butter

What you will need:

- ☐ heavy whipping cream
- ☐ empty yogurt cup and lid
- ☐ tape
- ☐ biscuit
- ☐ plastic knife
- ☐ honey

Fill a clean yogurt cup half full with whipping cream. Tape the lid shut. Shake for 3 to 5 minutes. Open the cup and scoop out the chunks of butter. For a different flavor, add some honey to the butter and spread it on a biscuit.

These exercises are simple and easy to set up.

What you will need:

☐ piece of rope

Optional items:

☐ ruler or other thin object, such as a pencil

☐ cardboard

☐ beanbag

 Rope Snake

Tie one end of a piece of rope or a jump rope to a pole or table leg. Have the child make a snake by moving the rope back and forth. Tell her to make the snake slither fast, shaking the rope back and forth quickly. Then have the snake move slowly. Tighten the slack on the rope to make skinny shakes. Give the rope more slack, so the child has to move her arms farther back and forth to make big shakes.

 ## Rope Circles

Make circles with the rope. Sing the following to the tune of "London Bridge."

Make a circle, make it round, make it round, make it round.

Make a circle, make it round, make it round.

Variations:

Make the circle big.

Make the circle small.

Make the circle fast.
(And sing the song quickly!)

Make the circle slow.
(And sing the song slowly.)

 ## Pull It Down

Tie a piece of rope to a sturdy tree or pole and play tug-of-war. Can you try to "pull down" the pole?

Extend It!

Tug-of-War

Play tug-of-war with your child. Tie a piece of yarn or cloth to the middle of the rope as a marker, and place a ruler or other thin object on the ground between you. Whoever pulls the marker over the ruler wins.

Pull Me

You and the child both hold opposite ends of a rope. Take turns pulling each other around the house. Be careful not to pull your partner into anything!

Balance Beam

Lay a rope on the ground and use it as a balance beam.

 ## Face Shake

Cut out a large cardboard circle with a hole in the middle. Draw two circles for the eyes and draw a mouth. The hole in the center is the nose. Tie one end of a rope to a pole or table leg. Thread the other end of the rope through the "nose" in the cardboard face. Have the child hold the free end of the rope and start shaking the face. See how long it takes the face to move to the child.

 ## Beanbag Jump

Tie a beanbag to the end of a piece of rope. Swing the beanbag in a circle about 3 inches off the ground. Let the child jump over the beanbag as it approaches him. Switch places and have the child swing the beanbag in a circle while you jump over the rope.

OTHER GROSS-MOTOR ACTIVITIES

 ## Punching Bag

This is very simple to set up and take down.

What you will need:

- ☐ plastic grocery bag
- ☐ newspaper
- ☐ rope or heavy string

Optional items:

- ☐ rubber ball
- ☐ fallen leaves

Have the child help you fill a plastic grocery bag with crumpled newspaper. Tie the plastic bag shut and hang it by stringing rope through the handles. Let the child punch away. For a different feel, try stuffing a bag with leaves or put a big rubber ball inside.

 ## Making Taffy

Kids love making their own candy. From start to finish, this will take about 2 hours. The taffy needs to be pulled for 10 to 15 minutes. However, I prepared the taffy ahead of time and let my kids pull it after it cooled. Doing it this way, the actual activity time with my children was only 10 to 15 minutes.

What you will need:

- ☐ 2 cups sugar
- ☐ 1 cup light-colored corn syrup
- ☐ 1 cup water
- ☐ 1½ teaspoons salt
- ☐ 2 tablespoons butter
- ☐ 2 teaspoons vanilla
- ☐ candy thermometer
- ☐ wax paper or plastic wrap

Except for the vanilla, mix all of the ingredients in a medium saucepan over medium-high heat. When the mixture boils, reduce the heat to medium, add the vanilla, and insert a candy thermometer. Continue to let the candy boil at a moderate rate, stirring occasionally. Try to keep the temperature at about 250°F. After about 40 minutes, pour the candy onto a buttered cookie sheet. Let the candy cool for about 20 minutes.

Have the child butter her hands. (I sprayed my kids' hands with cooking spray.) Help her twist and pull the candy until it turns a creamy color and feels very stiff, usually about 15 minutes. With buttered scissors, snip pulled strands of taffy into bite-sized pieces. Wrap the pieces in squares of wax paper or plastic wrap.

 ## Hot Lava

My brother and I played this when we were little. It's great for a rainy day.

What you will need:

- ☐ couch cushions
- ☐ towels

Take all of the cushions off the sofa and chairs. Scatter them on the floor within jumping distance of each other. Lay a few cushions farther apart and place towels folded with a narrow surface area (like a balance beam) between them, connecting the cushions. Tell the child the floor is hot lava, the cushions are islands, and the towels are bridges. Let him jump from island to island and balance on the bridges, avoiding the "hot lava."

Extend It!

Watch Out for Sharks!

Pretend the cushions are islands, the towels are bridges, and the floor is shark-infested water. Designate one cushion as the boat. Have the child rock herself on the boat, back and forth, trying not to fall in the water.

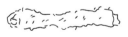  

 ## Making Sand

What you will need:

- ☐ rocks
- ☐ coffee can with lid
- ☐ tape

This is a good, nonedible alternative to "shake something" cooking. Fill a coffee can with several rocks and tape it shut. Roll the coffee can or shake it for several minutes. Open the can and see sand starting to form. For this to work best, use a softer type of rock. Broken pieces of brick work well.

 ## Laundry Basket Fun

Give your child a laundry basket. Make a trail of canned food, shoes, or stuffed animals around the house. Have the child push the laundry basket around to collect the items. Have a prize waiting at the end of the trail.

 ## Stocking Painting

What you will need:

- ☐ pantyhose
- ☐ sand or kitty litter
- ☐ paint (finger paint or other "kid paint")
- ☐ paper
- ☐ shallow container

Note: For this activity, to keep the paint from splattering too much, spread a large dollop into a pie tin or shallow container. You can also do this activity outdoors and use an old button-down shirt worn backwards as a smock.

Spread some newspapers on a table. Fill the toe of the pantyhose with ¼ cup of sand and tie a knot to create a small ball. Leave about 6 inches of pantyhose above the knot and cut the rest off. Put a large dollop of paint into a pie tin or shallow container. Let the child dip the ball in the paint then "bungee" the paint onto the paper. Holding the tail of the pantyhose, whack the ball of sand against the paper.

Blanket Parachute

What you will need:

- ☐ blanket or sheet
- ☐ teddy bear (or other stuffed animals)

Make Waves

Stand across from the child and grasp opposite sides of the sheet or blanket. Shake the blanket between you to make waves.

Chariot

Have the child sit on one end of the blanket. Pick up the other side and give her a "chariot ride," pulling her around on the blanket. Place stuffed animals and toys on the blanket and let the child give the toys a ride.

Bounce the Teddy

Place a teddy bear on the blanket. Stand across from the child and hold opposite sides of the blanket. Both of you shake the blanket to bounce the teddy bear!

Rock the Teddy

Place a teddy bear on a blanket. Stand across from the child, holding opposite sides of the blanket. Both of you swing the blanket back and forth, rocking the teddy bear on the blanket.

 Spoon Relays

What you will need:

- ☐ large spoon
- ☐ small potato
- ☐ cotton ball
- ☐ peanut

Place a bowl on one side of the room. Place a small potato, cotton ball, and peanut on the other side of the room. Give the child a spoon and have him walk to the potato, put it on the spoon, carry it to the bowl, and drop it in. Have him repeat this for the cotton ball and the peanut.

 # Tin Can Lantern

What you will need:

- ☐ washed and clean tin can
- ☐ votive candle
- ☐ paper
- ☐ pencil
- ☐ hammer
- ☐ nail
- ☐ tape
- ☐ water

Two days before doing this project, fill the can with water and freeze it solid. Cut out a piece of paper big enough to fit around the can. Have the child create a simple design by tracing around geometric shapes on the paper. Remove the can from the freezer and tape the paper around the can. Place the can on a folded towel. Use the hammer and nail to quickly punch holes in the can along the lines of the design. Then, remove the paper and the ice and place a candle inside the can. You can spray-paint the can when the design is finished.

Note: If the ice melts before the work is done, refreeze the can!

ACTIVITIES FOR BILATERAL MOTOR COORDINATION

Bilateral motor coordination is the ability of both sides of the body to work well together. Initially, children coordinate the left and right sides of their bodies symmetrically. Bringing both hands together to clap or catch a ball is an example of symmetrical coordination. Next, children learn to coordinate their bodies asymmetrically. Climbing steps by alternating the left and right feet is an example of asymmetrical coordination.

The following "acting out" songs are great for bilateral motor coordination:

- "Itsy Bitsy Spider"
- "Wheels on the Bus"
- "Johnny Hammers with One Hammer"
- "Father Abraham"
- "Hokey Pokey"
- "Mexican Hat Dance"
- "Chicken Dance"

Some other good activities include:

- jumping jacks
- wheelbarrow-walking
- martial arts
- gymnastics
- swimming
- yoga
- playing Twister
- playing "Simon Says"

 ## Marble Painting

What you will need:

- ☐ box top or cardboard tray
- ☐ marbles
- ☐ construction paper
- ☐ kid-friendly paint

Optional item:

- ☐ glitter

Cut a simple shape out of construction paper. Place the paper and a couple of marbles inside the box top. Next, sprinkle a few drops of paint onto the construction paper. Have the child hold the box top with both hands and roll the marble back and forth over the paint to decorate the construction paper. When the child is done, if you have glitter available, let him sprinkle some glitter over the wet paint, making sure he crosses the midline.

Extend It!

Amazing Planets

A larger version of this can be done with a plastic kiddie pool. Cut a large shape out of butcher paper and place it in the pool. Then sprinkle several spoonfuls of paint onto the paper and put a tennis ball inside the swimming pool. Have several children work together to tip the pool back and forth so the tennis ball paints the paper. We used this activity to create large planets to hang in our classroom.

ACTIVITIES FOR CROSSING THE MIDLINE

Some children have difficulty with crossing the midline. If you were to draw an imaginary line down the center of their body, they would have difficulty moving their hands, feet, arms, or legs across that line to the other side of their body. Along with a variety of sensory issues, my friend's son Heath had difficulty crossing the midline. When Heath colored pictures, he used both hands. He passed crayons and markers back and forth, using his left hand to color the left side of the paper and his right hand for coloring the right side.

At first, his mother thought this was wonderful—she thought he was ambidextrous. However, as Heath started school, problems with writing and reading began to emerge. School became so tedious for Heath that he often shut down and gave up.

I am happy to say that Heath has shown a lot of improvement through consistent therapy, and he is now reading. My son also had difficulty crossing the midline. Keeping one of his hands occupied by holding a squishy object often made therapy go much easier. We both really enjoyed the following activities.

 **Flour Racing**

What you will need:

- ☐ cookie sheet
- ☐ flour
- ☐ toy cars

Optional items:

- ☐ empty yogurt container with lid

This activity is easy to clean up if you place a plastic tablecloth under the cookie sheet. When finished, fold up the tablecloth and dispose of the excess.

Place a cookie sheet in front of the child. Sprinkle the cookie sheet with flour, so it barely covers the surface. Let the child make a "racetrack" in the flour with her finger. Make sure that she does not switch hands and that she crosses the midline. (You may want to give her a "squishy" to hold to keep one hand occupied.) Encourage her to make a large racetrack. Have her trace the outline of the track several times with her finger to make it wide enough for the car to race down. Once the racetrack is done, give her a small toy car to race on it. When the track becomes boring, smooth out the flour and make a new track.

Extend It!

Snow Day

Cut several holes in the lid of a clean, empty yogurt container. Fill the container half full of flour. Let the child sprinkle "snow" all over the cookie sheet. Remember to only let him use one hand, so he crosses the midline. Once it has finished "snowing," have him use his finger to clear the snow off the racetrack or street.

 ## Secret Pictures

What you will need:

- ☐ watercolor paints
- ☐ water
- ☐ paintbrush
- ☐ white candle or white crayon
- ☐ white paper
- ☐ cookie sheet

This is a fun classroom activity. Have kids make secret pictures for each other, then exchange the papers and let the kids reveal what their classmates drew!

With a white candle or crayon, draw a picture on a white piece of paper. Place the paper on a cookie sheet in front of the child. Have the child paint the paper with watercolors to reveal the secret picture. Make sure that the child does not switch hands, but paints back and forth across the midline.

CHAPTER 4

VISUAL ACTIVITIES

For Mimi, reading is torture. Along with a variety of sensory issues, she has attention-deficit/hyperactivity disorder. Her reading comprehension is poor because she must concentrate on tracking words so she doesn't lose her place instead of concentrating on *what* she is reading. This tracking problem also causes her to read the same sentence several times.

Although Mimi is a bright, fun-loving child, trying to get her homework done is a challenge every night for her and her family. Mimi receives both occupational and vision therapy and has improved significantly. Her parents are truly incredible! For kids like Mimi, sensory therapy as well as vision therapy may be warranted.

 Homemade Tops

This simple activity fascinates young children the first time they do it.

What you will need:

- ☐ paper plate
- ☐ colored pens or crayons
- ☐ pencil

Have the child draw red, yellow, and blue dots on a plate. Push a pencil through the center of the plate. Spin the plate on the pencil, and rings of different colors appear.

Extend It!

Draw pictures or different shapes on a paper plate to see what will happen when you spin it.

 Planetarium

What you will need:

- ☐ cereal box
- ☐ pencil
- ☐ two flashlights
- ☐ construction paper (dark and bright colors)
- ☐ scissors
- ☐ black marker

Punch several holes in an empty cereal box. Place the first flashlight inside the cereal box and turn off any lights in the room. Turn on the flashlight and enjoy looking at the "stars" together.

When you've turned the lights back on, cut a simple rocket-ship shape out of a piece of dark paper. (The rocket should be small enough to fit on the second flashlight lens.) Take off the lens of the second flashlight, and tape the rocket on the lens. Use a black indelible marker to color the inside of the reflective surface around the bulb black. Put the lens back on the flashlight. Turn the lights off again, and switch on the first flashlight inside the cereal box. Give the child the second flashlight with the rocket shape on it. Turn on the child's flashlight and have him "fly" the rocket through the stars.

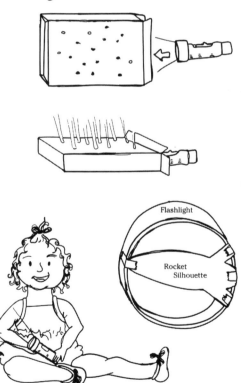

Flashlight

Rocket
Silhouette

 ## Rocket Tag

What you will need:

- [ ] construction paper (a dark color)
- [ ] scissors
- [ ] tape
- [ ] two flashlights

Use two pieces of dark paper to make two simple rocket-ship shapes. Tape the rockets to the lenses of two flashlights. Give a flashlight to your child, then turn off the lights in the room. Switch on both flashlights, and you and your child can play rocket tag. If your child likes trains or dinosaurs, you can play train tag or dinosaur tag instead—whatever is most interesting to him.

 ## Space Exploration

Cut out several brightly colored circles for planets and tape them to the walls. Turn out the lights. Using the "flashlight rocket" you made for the previous activity, let the child "fly" the rocket around the darkened room to find the planets on the walls.

 **Drop It Game**

What you will need:

☐ plastic peanut butter jar, coffee can, or hat

☐ clothespins, crayons, or other small objects

Have the child stand over an empty peanut butter jar, coffee can, or hat and try to drop clothespins, crayons, or other small objects into the container.

Extend It!

Place a coffee can, peanut butter jar, or hat on the ground. Have the child stand a few feet from it and try to throw small objects into it, such as pebbles, buttons, nuts, or dried beans.

Beanbag Toss

What you will need:

- ☐ beanbags or "squishies"
- ☐ cardboard box

Optional items:

- ☐ small, medium, and large boxes
- ☐ several large hats

Cut several differently sized holes in the box. Encourage the child to toss beanbags through the holes.

Variation 1

Place small, medium, and large boxes inside of each other. Assign 10 points to the small box, 5 points to the medium box, and 1 point to the large box. Have the child throw beanbags into the boxes. See how many points a child can get with five throws.

Variation 2

Scatter several large hats on the floor. Encourage the child to stand about 2 feet from the hats and try to throw the beanbags into the hats.

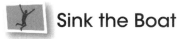 ## Sink the Boat

What you will need:

- [ ] water
- [ ] large plastic container
- [ ] small plastic container (such as a margarine cup)
- [ ] pennies or other small objects to toss

Fill the larger container with water. Place the smaller plastic container on top of the water, so it floats. Toss pennies into the boat until it sinks. You can also sink the boat with toy cars or pebbles.

 ## Koosh Catch

What you will need:

- [ ] plastic milk jug
- [ ] Koosh ball
- [ ] string
- [ ] scissors

Thoroughly clean a plastic milk jug and cut out the bottom. Tie one end of a string to the Koosh ball and the other end to the handle of the milk jug. Turn the jug over, throw the Koosh ball into the air, and try to catch it in the jug!

 **Block Bowling**

What you will need:

- ☐ 10 cardboard blocks or empty 2-liter bottles
- ☐ ball

Set up the cardboard blocks or empty bottles in a triangular formation, like bowling pins. Give the child a ball and let her roll the ball at the "pins" to knock them down.

 **Block Relay**

What you will need:

- ☐ cardboard or wooden blocks

Have the child stand the blocks up on their ends in a line, like dominoes. Push over the first block and see if they will all fall down to make a block relay. Let the child experiment with differently sized blocks, setting the distances farther apart.

 **I Spy**

Look around the room and pick out an object (something obvious). Say, "I spy with my little eye something that is..." and describe the object until the child can pick out what you're describing.

 ## Memory "I Spy"

Place several cards from the Memory game onto the table with the pictures facing up. Say, "I spy with my little eye something that is..." and describe a card until the child chooses the card you are describing. The better she gets at the game, the more cards you can set on the table.

 ## Ball Bounce

What you will need:

- ☐ large box
- ☐ bouncy ball

Have the child stand approximately 3 feet from the box. Let her try to bounce the ball into the box.

Extend It!

- If the child is working on language or social skills, you can prepare a series of social questions to ask the child if she bounces the ball into the box.
- Move the line back to increase the challenge.
- Use differently sized balls.

 Skee Ball

What you will need:

- ☐ 15 clean yogurt cups
- ☐ individually wrapped pieces of candy
- ☐ pennies

Place the cups into a pyramid shape and put one piece of candy into each cup. If you don't have yogurt cups, clean cans with masking tape around the edges will work, too. (You can also use disposable cups, but they don't work as well.) Let the child stand a few feet from the cup pyramid. Give the child a penny and let him try to toss it into a cup. When a penny lands in a cup, let the child take out the piece of candy and eat it. If you don't want to play this game with candy, you can use goldfish crackers or Cheerios, or the child can earn points for prizes each time he tosses a penny into a cup.

Extend It!

- Stand further back from the cups.
- Try tossing different items into the cups, such as cotton balls or kidney beans.
- Add question cards to the cups. Each time the child tosses a penny into a cup, let him answer a question or ask a friend a question. After the child has answered the question, let him try again. Continue playing until all the questions are answered, or, if playing with more than one child, everyone has had a turn.

 Crinkle Ball

What you will need:

- ☐ wastebasket
- ☐ paper bag
- ☐ masking tape
- ☐ newspaper

Make a basketball by stuffing a large paper grocery bag half full with crumpled sheets of newspaper. Fold the top of the bag down and seal it with tape. Next, put additional masking tape all around it to help keep its shape. Now you have a lightweight ball that you can shoot baskets with! For the basket, place a plastic laundry basket, wastebasket, or empty cardboard box on the floor or on a chair.

Miniature Version

Use a wadded-up piece of paper or sheet of aluminum foil to make a ball. See if the child can toss it into a coffee can or wastebasket.

 Ring Toss

What you will need:

- ☐ wire hanger
- ☐ wad of paper
- ☐ string
- ☐ tape

Bend a wire hanger into a circle, tie a piece of string to one end of the hanger, and then use tape to hang it from the center of a doorway. Blue painter's tape works great—it's fairly strong and easy to remove, and it won't damage paint. Have the child stand a few feet away and try to toss a ball of paper through the ring.

Extend It!

- Move farther away from the ring to increase the challenge.
- If the child is working on language or social skills, prepare some question or discussion cards. Let the child pick a card each time the "ball" goes through the ring.
- For an extra challenge, make paper airplanes and try to fly them through the ring!

HELPFUL VISUAL GAMES, BOOKS, AND TOYS

- Memory
- Guess Who
- mazes
- dot-to-dot books
- I Spy books
- Lite-Brite

CHAPTER 5
AUDITORY ACTIVITIES

My son was terrified of sounds. I had to warn him before I vacuumed, so he could run into his room, close the door, and cover his ears. When I finished, I found him with his head under the pillow.

He covered his ears at the sight of dogs or fire engines, fearing the noise they might make. While covering his ears protected his ears, it did not help him develop his auditory sense.

He needed exposure to sounds, and the only way we could do this, while ensuring that he felt comfortable, was to initially let him control all of the sounds in our sound games. If I accidentally made my son uncomfortable, he would resist trying the activity again because it moved from being fun to being scary. As you begin these activities with your child, remember that slow and steady wins the race.

MUSICAL ACTIVITIES

 ## Make Shakers

Musical instruments like these are fun to make and play.

What you will need:

- [ ] any kind of container, such as plastic soda bottles or yogurt cups
- [ ] things to fill the containers with, such as beads, rice, buttons, paper clips, sand, or birdseed
- [ ] construction paper
- [ ] tape
- [ ] markers

Place a handful of beads, beans, rice, or other fillers into a container. Put the lid on the container and tape it shut. Decorate a piece of construction paper and tape it around the container.

 Make a Tambourine

What you will need:

- ☐ aluminum (disposable) pie tins or paper plates
- ☐ things to fill the container with, such as beads, rice, buttons, paper clips, sand, or birdseed
- ☐ stapler
- ☐ stickers or construction paper
- ☐ tape

Have the child fill a pie tin with a scoop of beads or other small items. Place another pie tin on top, creating a hollow space between the two containers, and staple the edges together. Have the child decorate the tambourine with stickers or construction paper. Cover the staples with a small piece of tape.

Homemade Drum Set

What you will need:

- ☐ several pots and pans
- ☐ wooden spoon

Place the pots and pans around the child. Give her a wooden spoon and let her pretend the pots are her drums and the wooden spoons the drumsticks.

 ## Musical Drawing

What you will need:

- ☐ music
- ☐ paper
- ☐ crayons

Give the child some paper and crayons. Instruct him to draw only while the music is playing. Start and stop the music, and see if he can start and stop with it. Try to vary the tempo of the music.

SOUND GAMES

 What's That Sound?

What you will need:

- ☐ small container with a lid, such as a yogurt cup
- ☐ several small items, such as beans, rice, gravel, paper clips, and cotton balls

Optional items:

- ☐ household objects that make noise, such as a glass and spoon or broom
- ☐ musical instruments, such as a drum or whistle

Set several small items on a tray. Place a few pieces of the same kind inside the container, without showing your child. Shake the container, and ask him to guess which object you have in the container.

Extend It!

- Select four different objects that make noise, such as a shaker cup with a small item in it, a glass and spoon, a broom, and a pot and wooden spoon. Have the child turn around with her back to you. Then make a noise, such as sweeping the floor, and see if she can guess what it is.

- Use four instruments to make noise, such as a tambourine, drum, whistle, and harmonica. Have the child turn around with his back to you. Make a noise, and see if he can guess the instrument.

- Have the child turn her back to you. Clap three times and see if she can copy you without watching. You can also stomp your feet, bounce a ball, cough, hiccup, or shake a rattle.

Sound Hide and Seek

Variation 1

For this game of hide and seek, use any kind of instrument that makes noise. The child who's hiding gets to hold an instrument and makes noise until she is found. Some instrument ideas include a whistle, a harmonica, a bicycle horn, and a pot and a spoon.

Variation 2

Have the child hide an object somewhere in the room. He must give you clapping clues as you try to find the object. The closer you come to the object, the louder the child should clap. The farther away you walk from the object, the softer the clap. Experiment with sounds—instead of clapping, the child can blow a whistle, play a harmonica, beat a pan with a wooden spoon, or whatever seems fun and comfortable to him.

Marco Polo (Land Version)

Blindfold the child and quietly position yourself somewhere in the room. Have the child call out "Marco." Each time he calls, you reply with "Polo." You do not move during the game. This continues until the child finds you. Make sure the room is free of clutter and obstacles first!

"When I Say Go" Obstacle Course

Set up a simple obstacle course. Describe to the child how to navigate the obstacle course. Have him touch the television, hop around a chair, take five steps backward, walk across some couch cushions, or whatever seems fun. However, the child has to wait until you say "Go." If he follows the directions before you say "Go," he has to go back to the beginning of the course.

Treasure Hunt

Hide a small trinket somewhere in the house. Give the child clues to find it. However, before she can follow the clues, she must wait until you say "Go."

CHAPTER 6
ACTIVITIES WITH SMELL

Josh loves to smell everything. While shopping at the grocery store, he picks up fruits, vegetables, meats, and boxed goods, smelling them all along the way. There is no such thing as a quick trip to the grocery store. What is a mother to do?

His mom's solution was to make an "interesting smell" necklace. He only wears it when they go grocery shopping. Since it hangs right around his neck, it keeps him occupied and allows his mother to get her shopping done. He doesn't tire of it quickly because he only gets to wear it on special occasions.

How and where one provides therapy is only limited by one's imagination. If you would like to make a smell necklace with the child you are working with, check out the cinnamon rubbings on page 122. You can rub pieces of sandpaper with cinnamon sticks, cut them into various shapes, punch a hole in them, and hang them on some yarn for your own "smell necklace" fun.

 ## Kool-Aid Play Dough

I have found that most kids are tempted to taste this. They can try it—it is edible—but it tastes terrible. When I know several children will be playing with the play dough, I place a small amount in a separate container. Before the children start to play, I tell them there is play dough for tasting and play dough for playing, explaining that although it smells good, it tastes awful. Then I ask if anyone would like to taste it. I let them taste the clean play dough if they want to.

What you will need:

- ☐ 1 cup flour
- ☐ 1 tablespoon vegetable oil
- ☐ 1 package unsweetened Kool-Aid
- ☐ ¼ cup salt
- ☐ 2 tablespoons cream of tartar
- ☐ 1 cup water

Mix the dry ingredients in a medium pot. Add the water and oil. Stir over medium heat for 3 to 5 minutes. When the mixture thickens and forms a ball in the pot, remove it, let it cool a bit, and knead until smooth. Seal it in a plastic bag and refrigerate it until it cools.

Cinnamon Dough

What you will need:

- ☐ 1 cup ground cinnamon
- ☐ 1½ cups flour
- ☐ 2 cups hot water

Optional items:

- ☐ rolling pin
- ☐ cookie cutters
- ☐ pencil
- ☐ string or yarn
- ☐ beads or beans
- ☐ wire hanger

Slowly add the cinnamon to the hot water. Then stir in the flour. Let the dough cool before kneading it. Use this dough just like any play dough.

Extend It!

Ornaments

Roll the dough flat with a rolling pin. Cut out shapes with a cookie cutter. Decorate the shapes with beans or beads. Use a pencil to poke a hole in the shape. Let it dry for 2 to 3 days, then loop some string through the hole for hanging.

Make a Mobile

Create several ornaments. Using different lengths of yarn or string, tie them from a wire hanger to make a mobile.

Aroma Pictures

This art project smells great. Have the child work on a cookie sheet, and use a glue tub to keep the project less messy. To make the glue tub, cut a ½-inch hole in the top of a small plastic margarine tub. Fill the tub with ½ inch of glue and put on the lid. Give the child a small paintbrush and allow him to dip the brush into the tub through the hole.

What you will need:

- ☐ coffee grounds
- ☐ herbal tea
- ☐ construction paper
- ☐ glue
- ☐ paper plates
- ☐ cookie sheet

Draw a simple rectangle for a tree trunk and an oval for the top of the tree on some construction paper. Place a few tablespoons of coffee into a shallow bowl. Allow the child to paint the tree trunk with glue and decorate it by sprinkling coffee grounds over the glue. Pour the excess coffee grounds back into the bowl. Tear open an herbal-tea bag and place the contents in another shallow bowl. Have the child paint the glue on the oval, then sprinkle on the tea to make the leaves of the tree. Lay it flat until dry.

You can also use potpourri to decorate the tree.

Extend It!

- Draw simple animals, like bears, to decorate with the coffee and tea.
- Use potpourri to decorate simple flower shapes.

Spicy Plates

To cut down on mess, use a glue tub (as described in the previous activity) and place everything the child will be working with on a cookie sheet.

What you will need:

- [ ] cinnamon
- [ ] cloves
- [ ] paprika
- [ ] pepper
- [ ] oregano
- [ ] curry
- [ ] paper plate
- [ ] pencil or marker
- [ ] glue
- [ ] cookie sheet

Draw lines to divide the paper plate into six sections. Have the child apply glue to each section and then sprinkle on a spice. Have the child tap off the extra spice into a bowl.

Cinnamon Rubbings

What you will need:

- ☐ cinnamon sticks
- ☐ sandpaper

Encourage the child to draw a picture on the sandpaper with a cinnamon stick.

Extend It!

Gingerbread Men

Cut a figure of a gingerbread man out of sandpaper. Let the child rub cinnamon sticks on it to give him his smell. Then decorate!

Cinnamon Necklace

After rubbing cinnamon on the sandpaper, cut the paper into several small shapes. Then punch a hole near the top of each shape, and thread a piece of yarn through them. Tie a knot in the yarn to form a necklace that will fit over the child's head. This way, she can smell the spicy sandpaper while wearing the necklace.

More Smells

To make a necklace with a variety of smells, you can also rub the sandpaper with ginger, dried citrus peels, or hickory chips.

 Smelly Hide and Seek

What you will need:

- ☐ several sandwich bags
- ☐ cotton balls
- ☐ cinnamon
- ☐ vinegar
- ☐ vanilla extract
- ☐ lemon juice or extract

Take two cotton balls scented with several drops of a strong-smelling substance, like lemon juice, and place each one in its own baggie. Use several other scents to make pairs of baggies, just like the first set. Then, hide one cotton ball with each scent around the room. Give the child a baggie with the other scented cotton ball in it to see if he can find its smelly match hidden in the room. You can also use matching scented candles or potpourri packets.

Extend It!

Smell Hunt

Hide several baggies with different scents around the room and go on a smell hunt.

Toothbrush Fun

What you will need:

- ☐ toothbrush
- ☐ toothpaste
- ☐ cookie sheet
- ☐ water

Optional items:

- ☐ toys
- ☐ tubes of toothpaste with different flavors

Squirt some toothpaste onto a cookie sheet. Mix in a little water with the toothbrush. Let the child scrub the cookie sheet with the toothpaste.

Extend It!

Clean Something

Give the child some toys to clean with the toothbrush and some toothpaste.

Smell It

If your child has a strong need to smell, use different types of toothpaste, such as mint, bubble gum, or berry, and let her smell it as she scrubs.

 Smelly Wood

Adding dish soap to this homemade paint makes it easier to clean up.

What you will need:

- ☐ wood
- ☐ Kool-Aid
- ☐ paintbrush
- ☐ water
- ☐ cookie sheet

Optional items:

- ☐ sandpaper of differing grades

Kool-Aid stains easily, so when you set up this project, spread several sheets of newspaper on a table first. Mix a package of Kool-Aid and a squirt of dish soap with ½ cup of water to create "paint." Place the paint, a paintbrush, and a piece of wood on a cookie sheet in front of the child. Allow the child to paint the wood. The wood will smell for days.

Extend It!

Sand It

After the wood is dry, give the child some sandpaper and let him sand off the paint. It will release the Kool-Aid smell. For variety, use different grades of sand paper, one that is coarse and one that is very fine.

 Coffee Paint

Add used coffee grounds to finger paints. Not only will children enjoy the smell, but they may like the texture, too!

Kool-Aid Paint

This paint smells great, but it will stain clothes. Add some sugar-free Kool-Aid powder to ½ cup water. Add a squirt of dish soap to make it easier to clean up. Use this just like watercolors.

Smell Adventure

Walk around the neighborhood and find different things to smell. Take in the scents of the trees, the grass, the flowers, and even the mud!

Walk around the house, and find different things to smell. Does one room smell better than another?

Smelly Bath

Fill a bathtub with water, and add scented bath salts, lemon peels, or cinnamon sticks for an aromatic bath.

 ## What's That Smell?

What you will need:

- ☐ tray
- ☐ a variety of things to smell, like the following:
- ☐ easier items—soap, lemon, peanut butter, a flower, oranges, bananas, chocolate syrup
- ☐ harder items—garlic, shaving cream, mustard, ketchup, vinegar, vanilla extract
- ☐ blindfold

Place the items in small bowls or cups on the tray. Blindfold the child and hold one item up to his nose. Ask the child to guess the items. If you are playing with more than one child, give the items to the children in a different order or add and delete items to keep the game challenging.

CHAPTER 7
ORAL-MOTOR
ACTIVITIES

James had multiple developmental delays. At 8 years old, he could not eat solid food. His diet consisted of yogurt, applesauce, and some baby food. Solid or slightly chunky food made him gag or throw up. He was often constipated and bloated. His diet was a serious health concern.

His family began doing oral-motor exercises while slowly introducing more textured food into his diet. James now eats spaghetti noodles. It is a long, slow road with some children, but many small steps lead to big accomplishments.

BUBBLE FUN

 Bubbles Galore

What you will need:

- [ ] dish soap
- [ ] water
- [ ] 20-ounce plastic bottles
- [ ] strawberry baskets
- [ ] wire hangers
- [ ] funnels
- [ ] pie tin

Fill a pie tin with water and some dish soap. If you have a wire hanger, bend it into a diamond shape to make a giant bubble wand. Dip the diamond shape in the pie tin to get a soapy film over the opening. Encourage the child to gently blow at the film to make a big bubble.

To make a bubble horn, cut the bottom off of a 20-ounce plastic bottle. Dip the larger, open end into the pie tin to get a soapy film over the opening. The child can blow through the mouth of the bottle to make a big bubble appear. Let the child experiment with the different devices and create new ways to make bubbles.

 Dancing with Bubbles

Turn on some music and blow some bubbles. Have the child try to keep the bubbles in the air by blowing them upward while the music plays.

Caution: This can get slippery indoors!

As a variation, the child can also dance with feathers. While the music is playing, the child must keep the feather in the air by blowing on it.

Bubble Factory

This is good, clean fun. You can do this outside or sitting at a table indoors. If at a table, place the bubble factory on a cookie sheet and have a towel nearby for easy cleanup.

What you will need:

- ☐ yogurt container with a lid
- ☐ straw
- ☐ dish soap
- ☐ water
- ☐ towel

Fill a clean yogurt container half full of water. Squirt a tablespoon or two of dish soap into the water and stir. Cut two small holes in the lid and place it on the container. Insert the straw in one hole. Let the child blow through the straw and watch the bubbles pour out over the top of the cup and down the sides.

If you are worried that the child will suck the bubble solution up through the straw, poke a few small holes 1 inch away from the top of the straw.

Bubble Wrapping Paper

This is a fun way to make homemade wrapping paper. If the bubbles get on a child's clothes, they may stain, depending on how much food coloring is added to the bubble water. Have the child wear a smock or old shirt. For a quick and easy smock, use a plastic trash bag. Simply cut a hole in the bottom of the bag for his head and a hole on each side for his arms.

If you are worried the child will suck the bubble solution up the straw, poke a few small holes 1 inch away from the top of the straw.

What you will need:

- [ ] bowl
- [ ] straw
- [ ] dish soap
- [ ] food coloring
- [ ] water
- [ ] paper

Fill a bowl half full of water. Add 2 or 3 tablespoons of dish soap and some food coloring. Place a straw in the bowl and have the child blow bubbles in the water. When lots of bubbles have accumulated at the top, place a sheet of paper on top of the bubbles. The bubbles will pop on the paper, making a beautiful circular design. Then, just let the paper dry.

OTHER ORAL-MOTOR ACTIVITIES

 ## Painting Trees with Straws

To cut down on the mess, place the paper inside a cookie sheet before starting.

What you will need:

- ☐ paper
- ☐ black or brown tempura paint (or other "kid paint")
- ☐ small dish
- ☐ eyedropper
- ☐ drinking straw

Optional items:

- ☐ small container
- ☐ water
- ☐ dish soap
- ☐ food coloring
- ☐ bubble wand

Fill an eyedropper with paint. Carefully drop a couple of spots of paint along the bottom of a piece of paper. Have the child blow at the paint through a drinking straw to make the tree trunk. Scatter some more paint above the trunk the child created, and have the child blow at it to make branches.

Extend It!

Fancy Tree

After making a tree trunk and branches, decorate the tree with "bubble leaves." Fill a small container with water, dish soap, and a few drops of food coloring. Give the child a bubble wand and let her blow bubbles onto the paper. The bubbles will pop on the tree branches to make leaves!

 ## Making Pinwheels

Blowing pinwheels is always fun—especially when you've made them yourself.

What you will need:

- ☐ paper
- ☐ glue stick or stapler
- ☐ pencil
- ☐ scissors
- ☐ pipe cleaner
- ☐ straw
- ☐ crayons or bingo dotters

Cut out a 5- to 6-inch square of paper. From each corner of the square, make a straight cut toward the center of the square. Cut to within an inch of the center. Have the child decorate the pinwheel with crayons or bingo dotters. Paste down every other corner (four out of eight corners) to the center of the pinwheel. You could also staple the corners instead of using glue.

With a pencil or the point of some scissors, poke a hole in the middle of the pinwheel. Run a pipe cleaner through the hole and make a little loop at the end in the center of the pinwheel, so the pinwheel will stay on. Behind the pinwheel, bend the pipe cleaner at a right angle, leaving about ½ inch between the back of the pinwheel and the bend so the pinwheel can turn but will stay on the pipe cleaner. To give the handle of the pinwheel added strength, run the pipe cleaner handle through a straw. Make a loop in the pipe cleaner at the bottom of the straw, so the straw is secure.

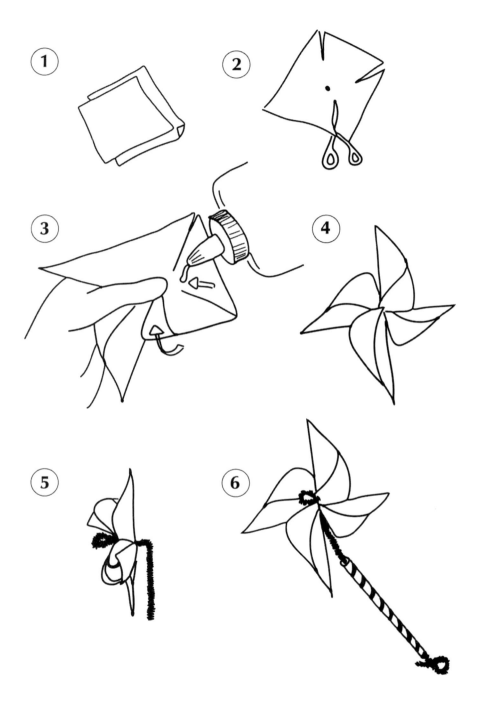

 On Your Knees

What you will need:

- ☐ balloons or small pieces of paper
- ☐ straws
- ☐ chalk, string, or rope

Use chalk, string, or a rope to make a starting line and a finish line. Have the child get on all fours at the starting line, bend down, and try to blow his balloon across the finish line. You can also give the child a straw to try to blow the balloon across the finish line. Small pieces of paper work just as well if you don't have balloons.

 Don't Breathe!

What you will need:

- ☐ a friend or two
- ☐ 2" x 2" pieces of paper
- ☐ straws
- ☐ chalk, string, or rope

Use chalk, string, or a rope to make a starting line and a finish line. Give each of the children a straw and a piece of paper. Tell them they must use the straw to suck up and hold the small piece of paper before they can start to move toward the finish line. Each time they drop the paper, they must stop where they are, pick up the paper, and suck in and hold it with the straw again before they start moving. The first one to cross the finish line wins.

 Coffee Slushie

What you will need:

- ☐ 2 cups milk
- ☐ 1 tablespoon instant decaffeinated coffee
- ☐ 3 tablespoons sugar
- ☐ measuring cups and spoons
- ☐ cups
- ☐ straws
- ☐ blender

Preteens love to feel older, which is why this drink is popular. Pour milk into the blender, then add ice to fill it. Next, add coffee and sugar and then blend until thick and frothy. Pour into cups and drink with a straw. Using crushed ice works best!

 Chewy Necklace

What you will need:

- ☐ yarn
- ☐ tape
- ☐ Cheerios or Fruit Loops cereal or Lifesavers mints

Cut a large piece of yarn long enough to make a necklace for the child. Carefully wrap a piece of tape around the end of the yarn to make an easy-to-hold "needle" for the child to string the cereal through. On the other side of the yarn, tie a big bow so that when the child laces the cereal, it will not fall off the other end. Let the child string the cereal onto the yarn. When she is done, cut off the tape, untie the bow, and secure the necklace loosely around the child's neck. If the child really needs something to suck on, instead of looping cereal you can use Lifesavers mints.

 ## Follow the Balloon

What you will need:

- ☐ balloon
- ☐ rope or chalk

Using chalk or rope, make a start line and a finish line. Line up behind the start line. Have the child blow up his balloon and then let it go while aiming it toward the finish line. Have him chase his balloon and blow it up again until it flies over the finish line.

Extend It!

Prepare question cards for kids to answer when they reach the finish line. Or, let them tell you one interesting thing about themselves when they reach the line.

 # Q-tip War

What you will need:

- ☐ Q-tips
- ☐ straws
- ☐ timer

Optional items:

- ☐ ping-pong balls

This is a fun game that my son made up. Divide into teams that are facing each other, no further than 5 to 10 feet apart. Give each player a straw and several Q-tips. Explain that the object of this game is to try to shoot your Q-tips at each other, and whoever has fewer Q-Tips on their side when the timer goes off wins.

Set a timer for 3 minutes. Now place the Q-tip in the straw and blow it as hard as you can at your opponent. (Some Q-tips are fluffier than others. If the Q-tip doesn't fit, just remove the cotton from one side.)

Extend It!

- Have everyone stand behind a line and see who can shoot their Q-tips the farthest.

- For a variation of this game, sit at a table or lie on the floor and use a straw to blow ping-pong balls at your opponent.

HELPFUL TOYS FOR ORAL-MOTOR ACTIVITIES

- any kind of whistle
- "blo pens"
- harmonicas
- pinwheels
- kazoos
- recorders

CHAPTER 8

FINE-MOTOR

ACTIVITIES

Fine-motor skills are precise muscle movements of the smaller muscles in your hands and toes. Frequently, children with SPD also have poor fine-motor skills. As with any muscle, it takes consistent, steady exercise of these small muscles to improve performance. The more exercise these muscles get, the fitter they will become. The key to getting your child to do lots of fine-motor exercise is to make it fun.

I did the following exercises with my son and the children I taught while I was a preschool teacher. They were usually a big hit with everyone.

 Color Mixing

This fun activity is easy to set up and clean up, if you make sure to place the ice cube tray inside a cookie sheet. However, food coloring may stain a child's clothes. Remember to roll up the child's sleeves or use a smock.

What you will need:

- ☐ food coloring
- ☐ water
- ☐ eyedropper or medicine dropper
- ☐ ice cube tray or empty plastic egg carton
- ☐ cookie sheet

Optional items:

- ☐ large block of ice
- ☐ salt
- ☐ coffee filters
- ☐ paper towels

Fill three compartments of an ice-cube tray or plastic egg carton with water. Put a couple of drops of food coloring in each compartment to make red, blue, and yellow water. Give the child an eyedropper and let him squeeze colors into the empty compartments and create new colors.

Extend It!

- Freeze a large block of ice. Place it in the kitchen sink or in a large pot. Pour salt over the block and encourage the child to squeeze the watercolors onto the ice with the eyedropper.

- Decorate coffee filters with colored water. Or, cut paper towels into various shapes to be decorated. Remember to line a cookie sheet with newspaper for easy cleanup.

 ## Popcorn Trees

For easy cleanup, use a large cookie sheet and a glue tub. To make a glue tub, cut a ½-inch hole in the top of a small plastic margarine tub. Fill the tub with ½ inch of glue and put on the lid. Give the child a small paintbrush and allow him to dip the brush into the tub through the hole.

What you will need:

- ☐ paper
- ☐ popcorn (popped)
- ☐ popcorn kernels
- ☐ green food coloring
- ☐ paper towels
- ☐ white glue

Optional items:

- ☐ brown marker
- ☐ other food coloring

Fill a bowl with one cup of water and the green food coloring. Dip the popped corn into the green water for a couple of seconds, then let it dry on a paper towel.

On a piece of sturdy paper, draw a rectangle (for the trunk of the tree) with an oval on top (for the branches). Let the child paint the rectangle with glue and decorate it with popcorn kernels. Next, encourage the child to fill in the oval area with glue and decorate it with the green popcorn.

Extend It!

Spring Tree

With a brown marker, draw a tree and some branches on construction paper. Dye the popcorn pink or leave it white. Have the child glue blossoms on the branches.

My Name

Write the child's name on a piece of paper and allow her to trace her name with glue, then decorate it with popcorn.

More Pictures

Color the popcorn different colors. Draw simple flowers, cars, trains, insects, or animals to decorate.

 Marshmallow Sculptures

If you don't have small marshmallows, just cut larger marshmallows into quarters to make smaller pieces.

What you will need:

- ☐ marshmallows, large and small
- ☐ toothpicks

Optional items:

- ☐ paper
- ☐ scissors
- ☐ raw veggies

Simple Spiders

Give the child one large marshmallow. Encourage him to stick the marshmallow with eight toothpicks for legs.

Animals

Make animal sculptures. To make a lamb, give the child a large marshmallow for the body, several toothpicks for the legs and a neck, and smaller marshmallows for the head and feet.

Extend It!

Snowflakes

Cut a simple snowflake out of a piece of paper. Lay the snowflake flat on the table in front of the child. Encourage her to make a three-dimensional snowflake with the toothpicks and marshmallows, using the paper snowflake as her guide.

Vegetable Sculptures

Provide several kinds of vegetables that can be eaten raw, such as sliced cucumbers, carrots, celery, broccoli, and cauliflower. Encourage the child to use toothpicks to assemble vegetable sculptures.

What's in My Purse?

What you will need:

☐ pairs of small common objects, such as crayons, keys, buttons, or baby socks

☐ purse

Put one of each item in the purse. Give the child an item and see if he can find the matching item inside the purse by using only his sense of touch. No peeking!

Extend It!

A New Version of "Go Fish"

Give two people a paper bag, each containing the same objects. The first player takes an object from her bag and asks the other player if he has the matching item. The second player reaches into his bag without looking, finds the match, and gives it to the first player. The second player takes a turn, asking for an object still in his bag. The first player gives him the item after she locates it by using only her sense of touch. Continue until all the items are paired.

"Can You Find It?"

Place three each of five different items (eg, three buttons, three paper clips, three clothespins, three cotton balls, and three quarters) inside a coffee can. Ask the child if she can find an item from each group without looking.

 **Bowl Relay**

What you will need:

- ☐ tweezers (tongs or clothespins can also be used)
- ☐ 5 bowls
- ☐ cotton balls
- ☐ popcorn
- ☐ small plastic animals
- ☐ dry macaroni

Optional item:

- ☐ music

Put a bowl with a few cotton balls in it on one side of the table. Place another bowl with some popcorn in it on another side of the table. On a third side of the table, place a bowl with small plastic animals in it. Place a bowl with dry macaroni in it on another side of the table. Give the child an empty bowl, and let him walk around the table, using the tweezers to place one of each item in his bowl. Make sure most of the items are easy at first. As the child improves his skill with the tweezers, add more difficult items to the relay.

Simpler Version

Put several cotton balls in a bowl and have the child use tongs to pick up the cotton balls and put them into another bowl. This can be a race if more than one child participates.

Extend It!

Musical Freeze Relay

Play some music while the child goes around the table, filling her bowl with items by using tweezers. When the music stops, she has to freeze.

Musical Relay Race

Play some music as the child walks around the table with a bowl and, using the tweezers, fills it with as many items as he can. When the music stops, it is time for him to move to the next bowl. Continue this until the child has been to each bowl.

 Cutting Fun

Practicing cutting is a great way to develop fine-motor skills. Some children may become frustrated while cutting because they close the scissors all the way and lose their place on the paper. To help with this, wrap tape around the inside of each handle so that the scissors don't close all the way.

What you will need:

- [ ] comics from the newspaper
- [ ] postcards
- [ ] old birthday or holiday cards
- [ ] construction paper

Optional items:

- [ ] paper plates
- [ ] glue
- [ ] tape

Place several different types of paper on the table and let your child cut out whatever she can dream up.

Extend It!

Make a Collage

Have the child cut several strips of different types of paper. Glue them to a paper plate to make a collage.

Hula Skirt or Silly Wig

Draw a line 4 inches from the top of a piece of newspaper. Have the child cut long strips of fringe, from the bottom of the newspaper to the line, for a hula skirt. Once the cutting is done, use some tape to fasten it around the child's waist.

For variation, use the fringe as a silly wig. Place the paper on top of the child's head, and use tape to secure it snugly. Tape the wig at the uncut strip, fringe sticking up.

 # Make a Banana Sandwich

What you will need:

- ☐ bananas
- ☐ plastic knives
- ☐ bread or vanilla wafers

Optional item:

- ☐ peanut butter

With a plastic knife, let the child cut some bananas into small rounds. Give the child two pieces of bread and have her spread peanut butter on one slice of bread. Then have her place a layer of banana on top of the peanut butter to make a sandwich.

For a treat, place a banana slice between two vanilla wafers to make a cookie sandwich.

 ## Marble Fishing

What you will need:

- ☐ marbles
- ☐ large bin
- ☐ small plastic toys

Optional items:

- ☐ blindfold
- ☐ ice cubes

Fill a bin with water, marbles, and a few small toys. Let the child fish out the toys with his fingers or his toes.

Extend It!

On a hot day, you can add ice cubes. To make it more challenging, blindfold the child and see if he can fish out the toys.

 ## Rapid Fire

This is a fun activity that has to be supervised. You can line up lightweight objects like balloons or ping-pong balls, but using candles makes it more exciting.

What you will need:

- ☐ squirt gun
- ☐ candles
- ☐ ping-pong balls

Line up several candles outside. Be careful to place them in a nonflammable area. Fill the squirt gun with water and let the child extinguish the flames. If using small birthday candles, stick them into a bagel, some Theraputty, or a ball of play dough so they don't fall over.

Extend It!

- Move farther back from the target.
- Use your other hand to aim and shoot.
- Try "trick" shooting—shoot under one arm, shoot under one knee, and look away from the target and try to shoot between your legs.

 ## Bumpy Bag

What you will need:

- ☐ pillowcase
- ☐ several objects

Place several objects in a pillowcase and hold it up so it's just within reach of the child. Allow the child to feel the sack for a few minutes. Then let him guess what he thinks is inside. Is it a toothbrush, ball, or flashlight? Any common objects will work.

 ## Bet You I Can Walk through a Piece of Paper

What you will need:

- ☐ scissors
- ☐ paper
- ☐ ruler

To introduce this activity, simply state, "I bet you I can walk through a piece of paper." Inevitably the child will insist that you can't do it. To start, fold a piece of paper in half the long way, making an 11 x 4-inch rectangle. Unfold the paper, and poke a hole with the scissors on the middle crease about an inch from the end. Cut the paper down the middle crease, and stop an inch from the other end. Now, refold the paper along the same crease, and start making alternating cuts from side to side, stopping about ½ inch from each end. Continue cutting all the way down, alternating directions, until you've got about an inch left at the bottom. Carefully pull the strips apart, and you will have a large circle that you can walk through!

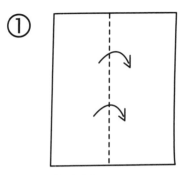

① Fold longways.

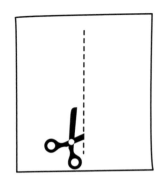

② Open and cut along crease, leaving 1 inch at both ends.

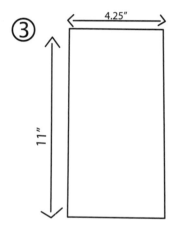

③ 4.25"

11"

Fold again.

④ Make alternating cuts, from edges to center fold (don't cut all the way through).

⑤ Open up and "walk" through.

HELPFUL FINE-MOTOR GAMES AND TOYS

- Operation
- Battleship
- Ker-Plunk
- Yahtzee
- Cootie
- Hi Ho Cherry-O
- Lite-Brite
- Tinker Toys
- Duplos
- Legos
- Lincoln Logs
- Lacing cards
- Pegs and peg boards
- Colorforms or stickers
- Puzzles and tangram puzzles
- Chinese checkers

About the Author

Every day offers an opportunity to help someone learn and grow. As a national speaker, writer, and the founder of National Autism Resources, Bonnie has a passion for sharing practical tools to help educate and nurture individuals with special needs. She has been married for 17 years and has two children, one of which has autism and SPD. She lives in Benicia, California.

Resources

Sensory World, a proud division of Future Horizons, is the world's largest publisher devoted exclusively to resources for those interested in Sensory Processing Disorder. They also sponsor national conferences for parents, teachers, therapists, and others interested in supporting those with Sensory Processing Disorder. Visit *www.sensoryworld.com* for further information.

Sensory World
1010 N Davis St
Arlington, TX 76012

Phone: (877) 775-1896 or (682) 558-8941
Fax: (682) 558-8945
info@sensoryworld.com
www.sensoryworld.com

Additional Resources

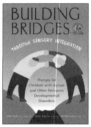

Paula Aquilla, Ellen Yack, & Shirley Sutton
Building Bridges through Sensory Integration,
2nd edition
www.sensoryworld.com

Britt Collins & Jackie Olson
Sensory Parenting: From Newborns to Toddlers—
Everything Is Easier When
Your Child's Senses Are Happy!
www.sensoryworld.com

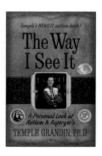

Marla S. Fisch
Sensitive Sam: A Sensitive Story with
a Happy Ending for Parents and Kids!
www.sensoryworld.com

Dr. Temple Grandin
The Way I See It and *Thinking in Pictures*
www.fhautism.com

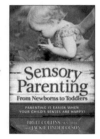

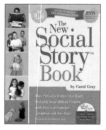

Carol Gray
The New Social Story Book
www.fhautism.com

Jennie Harding
Ellie Bean, the Drama Queen
www.sensoryworld.com

David Jereb & Kathy Koehler Jereb
*MoveAbout Activity Cards: Quick and Easy Sensory
Activities to Help Children Refocus,
Calm Down or Regain Energy*
www.sensoryworld.com

Joan Krzyzanowski, Patricia Angermeier,
& Kristina Keller Moir
Learning in Motion: 101+ Fun Classroom Activities
www.sensoryworld.com

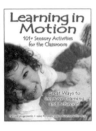

Jane Koomar, Stacey Szklut, Carol Kranowitz, et al
*Answers to Questions Teachers Ask about Sensory
Integration*
www.sensoryworld.com

Aubrey Lande & Bob Wiz
Songames™ for Sensory Integration (CD)
www.sensoryworld.com

Rebecca Moyes
*Building Sensory Friendly Classrooms
to Support Children with Challenging Behaviors*
www.sensoryworld.com

Laurie Renke, Jake Renke, & Max Renke
I Like Birthdays…It's the Parties I'm Not Sure About!
www.sensoryworld.com

John Taylor
Learn to Have Fun with Your Senses!
The Sensory Avoider's Survival Guide
www.sensoryworld.com

Kelly Tilley
Active Imagination Activity Book:
50 Sensorimotor Activities to Improve
Focus, Attention, Strength, & Coordination
www.sensoryworld.com

Carol Kranowitz
The Out-of-Sync Child, 2nd ed; *The Out-of-Sync Child Has Fun*,
2nd ed; Getting Kids in Sync (DVD featuring the children of St.
Columba's Nursery School); *Growing an In-Sync Child*; Sensory
Issues in Learning & Behavior (DVD); *The Goodenoughs Get in Sync*;
Preschool Sensory Scan for Educators (Preschool SENSE) Manual and
Forms Packet ~ www.sensoryworld.com

Index

D

dance and movement, 69–70.
    See also gross-motor activities;
    music activities
*Diagnostic and Statistical Manual
    of Mental Disorders* (APA), 8
diet, sensory, 15–16
"don't breathe" activity, 137
doughnuts, 40
drop it game, 99
drumming, 70, 111
dyspraxia, 5–6

E

edible activities. *See also* recipes
    ant farm, 38
    banana sandwich, 152
    coffee slushie, 138
    doughnuts, 40
    finger paint, 28
    marshmallow sculptures, 147
    no-cook cooking, 37–41
    peanut butter cookies, 37
    "shaking" recipes, 75–77
    taffy, 82
    watermelon slushie, 39
educational services, 9–13
eggshell pictures, 47

F

face shake activity, 80
feather activities, 63
fine-motor activities, 143–157.
    See also gross-motor activities;
    tactile activities

banana sandwich, 152
bowl relay, 149–150
bumpy bag, 155
color mixing, 144
marble fishing, 153
marshmallow sculptures, 147
overview of, 143
paper, walking through,
    155–156
popcorn trees, 145–146
purse activity, 148
rapid fire, 154
resources, 157
scissor cutting, 151, 155–156
finger paint, 20–21, 25–26, 28
flour racing, 93
follow the leader, 62
food. *See* edible activities; recipes
freeze dance, 69

G

glue tubs, 120, 145
grape stomp, 55
gross-motor activities, 57–94.
    See also crossing the midline
    activities; fine-motor activities
    animal movement, 61
    with balloons, 71–72
    for bilateral motor
        coordination, 60, 89–91
    blanket parachute, 86
    for crossing the midline,
        92–94
    games, 60, 62, 63, 64, 83,
        84, 87
    with music and dance, 69–70

Q

therapists, 13–14
tissue paper activity, 50–51
toilet-paper dance, 70
toothbrush fun, 124
tops, homemade, 96
touch (tactile perception), 1–3.
    See also tactile activities
treasure hunt, 116
tree painting, 133–134

U
underresponsivity, 3–4

V
vestibular perception, 2–3. *See also* gross-motor activities
vision (visual perception), 1–3
visual activities, 95–108
    with balls and tossing, 100, 103, 104, 105, 106
    with blocks, 102
    drop it game, 99
    with flashlights, 97, 98
    "I spy" games, 102–103
    overview of, 95
    resources, 107
    sink the boat, 101
    tops, 96

W
watermelon slushie, 39
Web sites
    Sensory World, 161
    SPD Network, 13
    "Wheels on the Bus," 67